What Christian leaders are saying . . .

You won't regret the time you spend reading Eddie Rasnake's book. I count it a privilege to know him personally and work with him. His book will help you read the signposts of decisions correctly and properly.

Dr. Spiros Zodhiates
President, AMG International
Host, "New Testament Light"

As I travel around our world, I find Christians everywhere asking the all-important question, "What is God's will?" Eddie Rasnake's book provides sound scriptural direction in helping us find the answer to that question. I highly recommend it.

Dr. Bill Bright, President and Founder
Campus Crusade for Christ

Eddie Rasnake has given us clarity and insight along with solid scriptural examples of how God leads people as we approach the twenty-first century. His book has already been helpful to me personally, and I expect the same result in the lives of multitudes.

Dan Hayes, Author
Director, National Collegiate Prayer Alliance

Throughout my ministry of forty-one years, I have never read anything more fresh and enlightening than this book of knowing and living the will of God.

Rev. Bill Stafford, Evangelist
Director, International Congress on Revival

Those who seek to do God's will often make decisions with lifelong impact. The tendency is to want to see our names written in the sky along with specific instructions as to what to do. Eddie Rasnake helps young and old alike understand how to know God's will by seeking God's way.

Frank Brock
President, Covenant College
Lookout Mountain, Georgia

As a minister for more than thirty years, I have often sought to give counsel about God's will. I have never found a book as clear, concise and simple as Eddie Rasnake's book. It was a blessing to me to read it, and I recommend it to all.

Dr. Robert C. Burch, Senior Pastor
Calvary Baptist Church
Knoxville, Tennessee

Fresh, original, imaginative — and biblical — were the words that came to mind as I read *What Should I Do, Lord?* Easy reading makes the principles accessible even to the newest Christian.

Ron Dunn, Author, Conference Speaker
Director, LifeStyle Ministries

I highly recommend this book not only to the new believer struggling with the topic for the first time, but also to the older saint who would like a fresh look at how to discover God's will. Eddie has a non-threatening way of saying hard things, and he deftly and practically presents biblical truth in a palatable, memorable style. It is a refreshing look at a well-worn subject.

Jan Silvious, Author
Host, "Jan's Journal" (on Moody radio)

What Should I Do, Lord?

EDDIE RASNAKE

Here's Life Publishers

First Printing, August 1992

Published by
HERE'S LIFE PUBLISHERS, INC.
P. O. Box 1576
San Bernardino, CA 92402

Library of Congress Cataloging-in-Publication Data
Rasnake, Eddie.
    What should I do, Lord? : following the signs that to God's
will / Eddie Rasnake.
        p.   cm.
    ISBN 0-89840-356-1
    1. Christian life—1960- . 2. God—Will. 3. Communication—
Religious aspects—Christianity. I. Title.
BV4501.2.R328   1992
248.4—dc20   92-19372
                                            CIP

Upon the release of each new book, Here's Life Publishers sponsors the planting of a tree through Global ReLeaf™, a program of the American Forestry Association.

Scripture quotations are from *The New American Standard Bible,* © The Lockman Foundation 1960, 1962, 1963, 1968, 1971, 1972, 1975, 1977.

Cover design by David Marty Design

For More Information, Write:
L.I.F.E.—P.O. Box A399, Sydney South 2000, Australia
Campus Crusade for Christ of Canada—Box 300, Vancouver, B.C., V6C 2X3, Canada
Campus Crusade for Christ—Pearl Assurance House, 4 Temple Row, Birmingham, B2 5HG, England
Lay Institute for Evangelism—P.O. Box 8786, Auckland 3, New Zealand
Campus Crusade for Christ—P.O. Box 240, Raffles City Post Office, Singapore 9117
Great Commission Movement of Nigeria—P.O. Box 500, Jos, Plateau State Nigeria, West Africa
Campus Crusade for Christ International—100 Sunport Lane, Orlando, FL 32809, U.S.A.

*This book is dedicated to
my wife Michele,
God's greatest blessing to me,
and continuing proof that His will is
good, acceptable, and perfect.*

Contents

□□□

Acknowledgments

□□□

The stories and illustrations in this book are true and come from the author's own counseling situations. To respect the confidentiality and privacy of the individuals involved, names and certain identifying circumstances of the stories have been changed.

I would like to acknowledge chronologically the men God used to build into my life and make me who I am: Blake Cornett, my grandfather; Mack Card, who led me to Christ; Rev. Don Strother; Dr. Paul Walwick; Earle Chute; Gary Wyatt; Terry Spinelli; Dorsey McIntosh; Dan Hayes; Tom Oyler; Dr. Robert C. Burch; Wayne Barber; and Dr. Spiros Zodhiates. These men of God have made many investments in my life. May those investments continue to bear fruit.

1

Beginning the Process

❑❑❑❑❑

Julie tossed nervously in her bed, unable to sleep. Her mind raced as she tried to process her circumstances. Tonight as they sat in the dorm lobby talking, Bill had brought up the subject of marriage again. Their relationship is moving so fast, yet she feels she is in love with him. Maybe he *is* the one. But she just isn't sure. "What should I do, Lord?" she implores in prayer.

Sam nervously broke the lead of his pencil as he scratched meaninglessly at the project he was working on. He couldn't seem to focus on the work. His mind kept leaping back to the decision he had to make. The job offer seemed to be too good to be true: a $10,000 raise, his own secretary, a company car, and a job he felt he could really sink his teeth into. But it would mean moving halfway across the state, leaving all their friends, their family and their church. In addition it would uproot the kids from school, and Steve had just been accepted on the varsity football team. Beads of perspiration speckled Sam's brow as he pleaded, "What should I do, Lord?"

Danny's stomach churned in knots as he ineptly played with the food on his plate. He had no appetite for it even though Mom had fixed his favorite dinner. Graduation was only three weeks away and he still had no idea what he was going to do this summer, let alone with the rest of his life. Should he go on to graduate school and get a master's degree, or should he accept his dad's offer and take a position in the family business? Deep in his heart he really wanted to join his friend Dave and do missions work in South America, but he knew there was no way his parents would go for that. Under his breath he mouthed the words in a heartfelt cry: "What should I do, Lord?"

"What should I do, Lord?" Have you ever found yourself praying that prayer? If you are like me, it has shown up in your silent conversations more than once. Often, we quietly wish God would just write His will in big letters across the sky or speak to us audibly. Perhaps like me, you are pretty leery of those who say "God told me . . . " but at the same time you wish He also would "tell" you.

We grapple with God's will because, first of all, we believe He knows what is best. But deeper than that, in our heart of hearts we don't want to suffer the consequences of making a wrong decision, so we want God to make the decision for us. He doesn't always do that as neatly as we'd like, but He does want to lead us, and contrary to the teaching of some, what we decide does make a difference.

The Scriptures are not silent about God's will. In fact, the subject comes up quite often. I don't believe the problem we sometimes have in discerning God's will is that He isn't showing it like He used to. It seems to me the problem is that we have lost sight of how God communicates, and we aren't looking for answers in the right places. In the pages ahead you'll find out where those right places are. This book doesn't offer "ivory tower" ideologies but practical, usable principles distilled from God's Word and explained on a grass-roots level. Don't worry, "The cookies are on the bottom shelf."

The pursuit of God's guidance is not some kind of spiritual Easter-egg hunt where God disguises His will and says, "Find it if you can." It is my conviction that the road to God's will is well-marked with signposts to direct us. But like traveling in another country, we have to spot those signposts and learn to read them, and then we have to choose to follow them.

The crucial first step in this process of discerning the will of God is *observation* (spotting the signposts). If we do not see the signposts God places before us, if we are not looking for them, we cannot expect to find God's will. But the process doesn't end there.

We may observe these signposts, but if our senses are not trained to *interpret* them (rightly understand what they mean), they are of no more benefit to us than Braille to someone who isn't blind.

Then, even if we do observe the signposts and accurately interpret them, they will not help us until we *apply* them (obey what they say).

Let me give you a good parallel: A stop sign doesn't protect you from wrecking your car if you don't stop at it. And to stop at it, you must first see it. Then you must understand what it means, and then you must act on it. God's signposts work the same way. The process breaks down if we omit any one of these parts.

Observation, interpretation, and application are a part of communication on any level. If these steps for seeking God's will sound like the process of Bible study to you, it isn't by accident. The Bible is God's recorded will, and — equally important to our process — it is God's communication to us. In the pages ahead you will learn how to connect with God in His communication process, how to interpret what He says, and, through practical application questions, how to evaluate your situation and act on God's will. I've laid the tracks for you but you'll have to drive the train.

Before we go any further, though, before we start identifying these signposts of God's will, we must consider some important preliminaries: We need to get God's perspective — we need to think rightly about His will.

What God's Will Is Like

Unfortunately, most of us operate from a woefully deficient picture of God and how He views us. Instead of seeing Him as the Good Shepherd and Loving Father, we tend to react toward Him as if He were the proverbial "gray-headed old man with a stick." We imagine Him looking out over the battlements of heaven for people who are having fun just so He can whack them and tell them to "cut it out!"

As author and speaker Dan Hayes puts it, often we are guilty of believing that to be in God's will means "hopping the first boat to Borneo and spending the rest of our life swabbing sores in some native hut." But I wonder how many of us, deep down, under our whitewashed veneer of spirituality, really believe God's will for our lives is good—even if we don't go to Borneo?

I am reminded of the old Quaker who in a moment of honesty with God said, "I'm not surprised You don't have any more friends than You do because of the way You treat the ones You have."

The Scriptures, however, paint a very different picture of God and His will. He is the "Father of mercies, and the God of all comfort" (2 Corinthians 1:3), the Good Shepherd who lays down His life for His sheep (John 10:11), the Sovereign God who loves us so much He calls us His children (1 John 3:1), the Father who gives only good gifts (James 1:17)—and the list goes on and on. God's desire for us is not to make us miserable but to make our lives meaningful and to make us more like Himself.

In Romans 12:2 we see a clear description of God's will: "that which is good, and acceptable, and perfect." Think about that. God's will for you personally really is good. His will is acceptable (the Greek word means "well-pleasing, agreeable"), and it is perfect (having the idea of "that which meets the need of the person"). God's will for you and me is all that and more.

Let's be honest with each other. Haven't you sometimes struggled with wanting to choose your own will over God's? I have. Just think how much it would help us in those situations if we really understood that His will, His specific desire for us in that circumstance, was good, acceptable, and perfect. Right now you may be seeking God's will. What a comfort to know with certainty that His will is better for you than your own will is!

Why We Need God's Will

Have you ever taken the time to ask yourself, *"Why do I need to know God's will?"* Probably not. That's not the kind of question a Christian is supposed to ask, but being able to answer it is of real benefit. It is the "whys" that enable us to consistently do the "hows." Perhaps the best single answer to that "why" question is found in Ephesians 5:15-17 where we are exhorted:

> Be careful how you walk, not as unwise men, but as
> wise, making the most of your time, because the days
> are evil. So then do not be foolish, but understand
> what the will of the Lord is.

The thing that differentiates the wise man from the foolish is that the wise man "understands God's will."

It is impossible for us to make the most of our time in these evil days without knowing God's will for us. Based on this we can safely say that God wills that we know His will.

In Colossians 1:9 the apostle Paul relates this same truth in a little different way. He prays that the Colossian believers would be "filled with the knowledge of His will in all spiritual wisdom and understanding."

In verse 10 he gives the reason for this prayer: "so that you may walk in a manner worthy of the Lord, to please Him in all respects." You see, it is impossible to walk worthy of the Lord or to please the Lord apart from discerning and doing His will.

The Promise of God's Will

We know we need God's will, but often I think we end up feeling like a donkey chasing a carrot on a stick: No matter how hard we try, we can't seem to catch it. The truth is, if we are seeking God's will and not finding it, the problem is likely on our end. Our Lord promises: "If any of you lacks wisdom, let him ask of God who gives to all men generously and without reproach" (James 1:5).

As you travel down the path toward God's will, pay special attention to the common mistakes people make, and you will avoid many a pitfall. This book offers no promise of divine skywriting or voices from the beyond, but if you follow God's principles, you *will* find His will. And in the process, you will learn more about how He communicates. I'll be honest with you. There are really two reasons I wrote this book:

First: I know what it feels like to grapple with God's will, and I want to help you find it.

Second: If I can walk you through the process in a practical way and help you succeed in hearing what God is saying to you now, I also will have moved you further down the road toward the future. Then the next time you need to know God's leading, the process will be easier for you. I don't want you just to know God's will; I want you to know also how to follow Him as a way of life.

Happy trails!

2

The Binary Trap

□□□□□

One of the most common things that trip us up in the process of discerning God's direction is what I call the "Binary Trap." Let me explain what I mean by that. When it comes to decision making, all too often we reduce the determination to only two options: an either-or, "binary" choice. That may not sound like any big deal, but slipping into this mode can send us speeding down the wrong road. The problem is, if we've come up with the options ourselves, both may be wrong.

As a sophomore in college I grappled with a decision that was important to me. I'd become a Christian as a freshman at a moderately sized state school in the South, and now as I grew in my relationship with Christ, I wondered if it might be better to transfer to a Christian college where I could deepen my knowledge of the Scriptures. I also played soccer, and at the particular Christian college I was interested in, the level of coaching and competition would be much greater than where I was. On the other hand, if I stayed, I could continue to reach out in ministry to those around me.

My approach to solving this decision-making dilemma was to ask God, "Should I stay at the secular school or transfer to the Christian school?" At face value this may seem fine, but I had already made a crucial mistake. I had limited myself to only two options: an either-or decision. While this type of decision may be easier to make than one with many options, I hadn't considered that possibly neither would be God's way of solving my problem. As a result, the decision became far more involved and emotional than it really needed to be.

After several weeks of agonizing and plenty of Alka-Seltzers, I finally sat down and tried to identify exactly what needs I was trying to meet. In this case, I sensed a need for a deeper knowledge of the Scriptures, and I desired to be where I could grow in my soccer skills and determine how far I could go with them. No problem there. Nothing is wrong with either of those desires. So the two primary relevant factors were:

1. Developing biblically

2. Developing my soccer skills

If that were you, what would you decide? Like me, faced with those two objectives and limited to those two options, you probably would decide to transfer to the Christian school. In this case, however, that wasn't God's will. I believe that if I had followed through and changed schools, I would have forfeited forever some of the most significant opportunities to minister that I had in my young Christian life. Although attending this particular Christian college would have deepened my knowledge of God's Word, I believe in some ways it would have hindered my applying it. The incredible opportunities to minister on a secular college campus are unparalleled in almost every other segment of our society, and God blessed me enormously as I pursued them.

So how did I make the decision? Through the counsel of a good friend, God showed me the binary trap I had placed myself into and I finally prayed, "Would something else meet these objectives better?"

How liberating that prayer was. Before very long I found out about a summer option that radically changed the whole process. My discipler shared with me about the Institute of Biblical Studies, a sort of summer-school seminary where I could deepen my knowledge of both the Old and New Testaments and of basic biblical doctrines. This particular summer, the Athletes in Action Soccer Team, a Christian post-college competition group, happened to be working out at the same location. I asked for and was given permission to work out with them for the summer.

I have no doubt that was God's will. This third option provided the benefits of a Christian college and then some, without requiring me to forfeit the ministry I had at a secular school. But finding it required that I break out of that binary trap.

So what got me into the binary trap? Two things, primarily. First, I hadn't prayed sufficiently nor had I adequately counted the cost. Second, I hadn't solicited counsel from others. Once I did those two things I was able to break free and find God's will.

How about you? Have you slipped into a binary trap? I realize sometimes that trap seems okay. For example, when someone asks you to marry him, isn't the decision really a yes or no decision? No, it isn't. That is why the binary trap is so sneaky. If someone asks you to marry him, you have at least three options: (1) Say yes and marry him; (2) say no and break up; (3) say wait, I'm not ready for this decision yet. Maybe you don't know him well enough, or there are uncertainties about your future, or whatever. Don't let someone else force you into a binary trap.

A recent book on the will of God suggested that the Lord really doesn't care whether I have pancakes or waffles for breakfast. As long as my decision doesn't violate some clear directive of Scripture, it really doesn't matter what I decide. While at a glance this may appear logical, it reduces decisions to a binary level. Although God may not have a preference in my choosing waffles or pancakes, He may prefer neither of the options I am offering Him. Instead, He may prefer that I eat something more nutritious. You see, our real need isn't simply God's *will* in a particular decision; we need His *wisdom* as well.

We need His perspective and His eternal value system to filter our decisions through. This book isn't simply to help you discover the decision God has already made for you; it is also to help you understand the principles of His Word and be able to follow them in other decisions He calls you to make.

Although in some situations the binary trap is okay, those times are a lot more rare than we think. If you struggle with this, there is hope for you. You can find the freedom and ability to discover God's will, even if it isn't one of your two choices. Remember, God wants you to know His will even more than you do, and He will show it to you. You just have to learn how to hear what He is saying. And you will! That's what this book is all about.

❑❑❑

Making It Personal

Why did you buy this book? Perhaps you picked it up simply to learn principles about God's will for your own interest and growth. Or more likely, you need to know God's will in your present circumstances. Why not take a few minutes now and identify a specific area that is troubling you? Then as you work through the principles in the pages ahead, you can focus them on something particular and apply the truths to your immediate need.

Don't worry if your first pass is a little sketchy; you will refine your skill as you work through the process.

The Decision to Be Made

(be as specific as possible)

Options Available to Me:

\#1

\#2

\#3

Other Pertinent Information:

3

Signpost #1

The YIELD *Sign:*
Settling the
Lordship Question

□□□□□

Betty tossed restlessly as the bedsheets tangled in knots of disarray. The glow of her digital clock glared the lateness of the hour, yet sleep was elusive. Her mind replayed the day's events like a video cassette. She had been excited when Sara called months earlier and asked her to be a bridesmaid. They had been roommates in college and even though their paths hadn't crossed much lately, it was still a special relationship. Now though, she wished she had never come. Oh, it was great to see the old friends and catch up, but she'd never before felt so conspicuously single. It seemed all her college chums were married and starting families.

"Come on, Betty, catch the bouquet!" they cheered as if trying to will her a mate. She hadn't really minded her friends' probing inquiry, "How's your love life?" at the time, but now her nerves pounded with the raw emotion of reality.

She wasn't getting any younger. The biological timeclock was ticking, especially if she wanted children. *In a few months I'll be thirty,* she thought. *Gee, that sounds scary. Maybe I'm just too particular. Maybe "Mr. Right" doesn't exist. Maybe it's time to start looking for "Mr. Okay." Bob certainly fits that bill.*

They had met at their Atlanta-based law office's Christmas party last year and had dated pretty steadily ever since. *He's reasonably good looking,* she mused, checking off his credentials. *He holds a good position in the firm's bankruptcy section . . . probably be a junior partner in a few years.*

Sure, he didn't really have the same heart for God as she, but he had started going to church with her sometimes, and lately he had been bringing up the subject of marriage. He seemed to want to settle down.

"Maybe that would mean less time running around and more time for God. Lord, I know he'll come to share my commitment to You," Betty exclaimed. She mouthed the words intensely as if trying to convince herself as much as God. "Lord, I want to be married . . . I'm tired of being single," she implored as she finally drifted off to sleep.

Several weeks later Bob surprised Betty with an engagement ring. In the excitement of the moment she silently prayed, "Lord, please bless our marriage." Had Betty found God's will, or had she simply decided what she wanted it to be?

YIELD

Perhaps the most important signpost on the way to God's will is the one which reads YIELD. One of the problems in people not being able to find God's will is an attitude that says, "Lord, show me what You want me to do so I can decide if I want to do it." This subtly communicates a perspective of us wanting the final say in the decision instead of leaving it to the Lord, and it suggests our mistrust of God's intent for us.

Often we doubt the words of Romans 12:2 that say God's will really is good. We want the right to put a "presidential veto" on anything that doesn't seem good to us or that we don't want to do. But God is not the U. S. Congress, and He will not be mocked.

He is not going to show us His will until first we settle in our hearts that we are willing to do what He says, whatever that is. God's will is not a choice to be made, but a command to be followed. Unless we are submitted to Him, He isn't going to waste His breath giving us orders. But, as that peerless theologian Lewis Sperry Chafer wrote in his book, *He That Is Spiritual* (Zondervan, 1918): "God is able to speak loud enough to make a *willing* soul hear" (emphasis mine).

Until we reach the point of yielding to God and trusting Him with each area of our lives, we will be like the doubting man of James, chapter 1: driven and tossed by the winds as a wave of the sea. James' verdict:

Let not that man expect that he will receive anything
from the Lord, being a double-minded man [lit. "two-
souled," a fence straddler], unstable in all his ways
(1:7,8).

If we want to find that good, acceptable, and perfect will of God that Romans 12:2 speaks of, we must first
settle the decision Romans 12:1 calls for:

I urge you therefore, brethren, by the mercies of
God, to present your bodies a living and holy sac-
rifice, acceptable to God, which is your spiritual
service of worship.

Although I realize it sounds a bit paradoxical, the
first step to finding God's will is yielding ourselves to it.
God wants us to answer yes, and then He will tell us what
the question is. We all realize that Jesus Christ is Lord.
What this passage shows is the need for us to let the Lord
Jesus Christ be Lord in us. Had Betty done that in her
decision?

What Does It Mean for Jesus to Be Lord?

We often see the "lordship of Christ over our lives"
as being like the role of the king or queen in governing
Great Britain. That country is presided over by the reign-
ing monarch, and yet Parliament, not the king or queen,
makes the rules, the decisions. Out of deference to this
monarch, a solid black line for the queen's signature appears in the lower right hand corner at the end of every
bill Parliament passes. The bill is then sent to Buckingham
Palace for her consideration, and by signing on the provided space, she gives her approval of the newly enacted
law. The interesting thing is, however, if she doesn't sign,
it is still law. She isn't the real lord of that country, the
Prime Minister is.

The British form of government is referred to technically as a constitutional monarchy. All too often, as in Great Britain's politics, we try to set up our lives as a constitutional monarchy. We have a position and place for a monarch, but we make the decisions and then we ask the Lord to approve our plans. The convicting reality I see, as I seek to follow the Lord, is that Christianity is not a constitutional monarchy. God does not want to approve of *my* plans; He wants my approval of *His* plans, and He wants me to submit to them. That is what it means for Christ to be Lord. Anything less is not true, biblical Christianity. As Jesus put it, "Why do you call Me, 'Lord, Lord,' and do not do what I say?" (Luke 6:46)

Barriers to Obeying This Sign

The two most devious and dangerous lures that keep us from obeying God's YIELD sign are *pride* and *self-centeredness*. Both are subtle in their approach and sneaky in their attack. If we don't watch for them, they will take us off the track of God's leading like a detour sign maliciously misplaced.

The life of King Saul (1 Samuel 15) quite graphically displays these characteristics. One of Saul's early tasks as king was to execute God's judgment on the Amalekites, the pagan tribe who ambushed defenseless Israel during the Exodus. Saul's assignment was to "utterly destroy" this heathen people, a severe but just punishment for their sinfulness. Deuteronomy calls this being "put under a ban," and it involved killing every living being — man, woman, child and beast — and destroying all their wealth and cities. Because that nation was so polluted by sin, nothing was to be spared.

Saul and his men were not obedient to this directive, however. They killed the people (except for King Agag), and they destroyed everything that was worthless. But the good stuff—the sheep, oxen, etc.—they kept for themselves. They were only partially obedient, which isn't being obedient at all. Notice what God says: "He has turned back from following Me, and has not carried out My commands" (1 Samuel 15:10).

Notice God doesn't say, "He only carried out part of My commands." Partial obedience is not obedience. If I obey God only when it doesn't conflict with my desires, I am not following God, but my own desires.

Why didn't Saul obey?

To start with, why did he spare King Agag? Well, in that culture, the king of a conquered army was a trophy to be brought back and displayed. The conquered king's humiliation intensified the victor's glory. Basically, that appealed to Saul's pride. He wanted to show off his success.

We see his pride also in his explanation of why he didn't obey: "Because I feared the people and listened to their voice" (verse 24). He was more concerned with how he looked before the people than with pleasing God (verse 30). We see his self-centeredness in his rushing to take of the spoils rather than being totally obedient.

The most telling aspect of this biblical vignette, however, is in how Saul responded once his sin was revealed. He displayed no remorse; he wasn't repentant about his sin. He wanted only to get out of the consequences (verses 25,30). Saul was proud instead of humble (in fact, after his victory, he even set up a monument for himself—verse 12). Because he did not have a heart after

God's heart (1 Samuel 13:13,14), he was rejected by God as king.

Pride

Pride often keeps us from yielding to God's will and way. Along with its ugly stepsister, vanity, pride comes into play in our hearts by subtly whispering, "You are too good for that." Oh, it doesn't say it so plainly, but that is the message just the same. Pride constantly sets limitations on what God's will can be. Vanity usually adds something about what people will think, or how something will look to others, or that such-and-such is beneath us, but both branches stem from the same tree.

Pride usually attaches conditions to God's will. It offers God a list of the things we are unwilling to do and demands that He adjust His will accordingly. It's as if we hid a mental list in our hearts somewhere. Pride tells God, "I'll go into any ministry You lead me, but You can't lead me to one where I have to raise my own support"; or, "I'll do whatever you want me to do, as long as I don't have to stay single"; or some other such statement. Could Betty have been affected by this in her decision?

A sober lesson from King Saul's life is this:

Yieldedness with conditions attached to it
is not yieldedness.

It is not deference to God's will and way, but to our own. Yieldedness includes all or it isn't yieldedness.

Self-Centeredness

Closely related to pride and vanity is simple self-centeredness. Often we are simply too concerned with our own interest to take thought of what is important to God. Self-centeredness says, "I want to do . . . " and holds that as the supreme litmus for evaluating God's will. You'll never find God's will until you settle in your heart that you want to do it whatever it is. If you are trying to figure out what God wants you to do, intending to then decide if it meets your criteria, you are simply wasting your time — and God's.

Several weeks after her engagement, Betty called me and asked if we could get together. As we sat and shared Cokes at a diner, Betty flashed a large sparkling diamond at me and smilingly said, "Congratulate me!"

She told me of her engagement to Bob and asked if I would marry them. At first I was surprised, but Betty seemed intent enough that I had to take her seriously. "I'd love to hear how God led you to this decision," I replied, and immediately the mood shifted.

I hadn't meant it as a confrontation, but Betty's countenance told me I had touched a nerve. She became fidgety and nervous, and she related vague reasons for this being a good decision. Then she closed it off with, "I just have a real peace about it."

In retrospect, I am confident it was the Lord's prompting that led me to respond by asking rather abruptly, "What if Bob isn't the man God wants you to marry?"

A mixture of shock and horror scurried across her face and she quickly retorted, "But I'm sure he is . . . he has to be!"

As I shared with Betty my interest in her welfare and my desire for her to experience God's best, I asked, "Honestly, how confident are you that this is God's will?"

After an awkward moment's hesitation, she confided, "Oh, I guess about 75-percent sure."

She seemed relieved as I began to share with her some principles about God's will, and I encouraged her to continue asking God to confirm His leading. I asked, "Betty, would you mull over what I've shared and hold the decision until you can be 100-percent sure?" I also encouraged her to get away for the weekend where she could give her undistracted attention to the decision at hand and to the Lord.

A week later the Betty I met with was a different person. Before a word passed her lips I could tell she had gotten her answer from the Lord. She began to relate to me her weekend with God; she had taken my advice and had asked God to line up the guideposts to His will. She shared with me the different counsel she had gotten and the time she spent "calculating the cost." She enthusiastically described her times in prayer and in the Scriptures, and how she applied the "sound mind" principle. "But the thing that turned the corner for me," she confessed, "was grappling with the YIELD sign."

Betty's eyes teared up as she began to share from her heart of coming to grips with the need to yield every area of her life to God's leading. "As I began talking honestly with God about various areas of my life, I realized that, though at one time my singleness had been yielded to God, in recent months I had taken it back from Him. I had begun to place marriage as a demand on God's will," she admitted.

As she realized this, she began to be honest with the Lord and tell Him of her desire to be married. She confessed, "Lord, in my heart being married has become more important to me than following You."

Joy shone on her face as she shared how in this spirit of intercession she asked the Lord's forgiveness. She again affirmed to Him, "Lord, I want to be in Your will even if that means singleness, because I know Your will is best. I know it will be good, acceptable, and perfect."

Once Betty yielded, and gave her singleness back to the Lord, she began to see Bob in a different light. Although he offered her a steady relationship and financial security, Betty realized he probably would never share her love for Christ. She recognized that, unlike her, he would not want to seek the Lord's will in the major decisions life would bring. Instead of encouraging her in her walk with Christ, he would probably discourage it. "What I really want," she confided, "is a husband who will lead me spiritually. Now I'm willing to wait on the Lord and trust Him to give me the husband He wants me to have. For the first time in ages, I have peace in my heart." She was experiencing that delicious sense of God's rest, and she quietly mused that this was worth waiting for.

□□□

Applying the Principles

Where are you in your search for God's will? Can you identify with Betty and her circumstances? Are you confused about a certain situation and faced with making a decision? Consider the following questions as you evaluate where you are, and apply this first and most essential principle in determining God's will.

An Evaluation

    1. Have I ever really surrendered my life to Jesus Christ as Lord and yielded myself to Him?

    2. Am I willing to do God's will in this situation no matter what that is?

    3. Are my motives affected by pride? (Am I unwilling to do something "beneath" me?)

    4. Are my motives affected by self-centered attitudes? (Am I placing my desires above God's?)

An Application

    As you seek to discern God's will, you will find yourself at a fork in the road. One direction is God's way, the other is your own. They may not always look like different destinations — sometimes the destination is the same — but the length of the trip and the means of getting there are different. You will never find God's will on the road to your own way.

    So now you must decide, but you also must realize your decision will have consequences. If you decide to go your own way, God, as your loving heavenly Father, will discipline you, and He will continue to place YIELD signs in your path.

On the other hand, if you choose His way, you must yield yourself to Him and trust that what He decides will be the best. But acknowledge this: You will never be disappointed, because God's will is filtered through His omniscience (He is all knowing); it is attended to by His omnipresence (He is ever present); and it is accomplished by His omnipotence (He is all powerful). Does your will have that much to offer?

Why not settle now that the Lord will be Lord in your life, and obey that YIELD sign? The following is a suggested prayer to affirm that decision. It isn't a magical prayer, and just saying the words won't change anything, but if you express this attitude in your heart to God, then you will be on the road to finding His will.

A Prayer

Dear Lord, I want You to be the Lord of my life. I yield to You and trust that You know what is best. Whatever You want me to do in this decision, I am willing to do. The answer is yes; now You tell me the question. Help me to find Your will, and whatever it is, I'll do it. Amen.

4

Signpost #2

The TELEPHONE *Sign: Prayer*

◻◻◻◻◻

"Have you decided what you are going to do during the summer, Eddie?" my friend asked. I was a freshman in college and Mack had led me to Christ a few months earlier. Since then I had leaned on his advice in spiritual matters, and in an informal way he was discipling me. He watched out for my spiritual welfare with the tender concern God gives a servant when He uses him to birth a new believer.

"What do you think about going on the beach project?" he asked with genuine interest.

A few days earlier he had told me about a summer mission project with the campus ministry we were involved in. One of these projects had been very significant in his spiritual growth, and he had challenged me to consider if this were something God would want me to do.

"I don't think I'm going to do that," I replied. "I'm leaning toward working at that Christian camp with Eric" (a mutual friend).

"Have you prayed about it?" he questioned.

"No, to be honest, I haven't." I guess it hadn't really dawned on me that I could ask God what He wanted me to do. As a new Christian, I knew God had a moral will for me, and I was trying to learn what pleased Him. However, I didn't really understand that He could lead me in the decisions of my life. It made sense though. After all, hadn't I read in the Bible to "pray without ceasing"?

"I'll take some time to pray about it before I decide," I assured him.

As I lay in bed that night, I remembered my commitment and began bringing the matter before the Lord. "God," I prayed, "I'm not sure what to do." I had pretty much decided to take a job as a counselor at the camp. It was situated in the Smoky Mountains near my home, and I loved the outdoors, so I was excited about the prospect of spending my summer hiking, camping and canoeing — and getting paid for it! The fact that it was a Christian camp was the icing on the cake. Surely God would be pleased if I did something Christian with my summer. It made sense to me. Trouble is, I hadn't asked God what He wanted me to do. As I realized that, I entreated, "What should I do, Lord?"

One near-fatal flaw we human beings have is our innate tendency to "lean on our own understanding." I'm not saying a Christian unplugs his brain when he seeks God's will, but the admonition of Proverbs 3:5,6 makes it clear that limited, finite human reasoning isn't adequate for all the decisions we are called to make. We are admonished to . . .

Trust in the LORD with all your heart, and do not lean on your own understanding. In all your ways acknowledge Him, and He will make your paths straight.

The Hebrew word for *lean* means "to support oneself." It doesn't mean that we don't use our own understanding; rather, it says that human logic alone is not sufficient to support us. We must lean on the Lord and ask His wisdom in all our decisions. Then He will direct our paths.

TELEPHONE

The second signpost we encounter on this road to God's will is the TELEPHONE sign. It is divinely designed to remind us of our need to "call home" — to ask our heavenly Father what to do and where to go. In Jeremiah 33:3 we read: "Call to Me, and I will answer you, and I will tell you great and mighty things, which you do not know." Some identify this reference as "God's phone number" because of its open invitation to "call to Me."

It is amazing how easily we forget to pray. Like I did with my summer decision as a new Christian, we often forget what a resource God is for our decisions. God's presence is always open to us. Though in Old Testament times the priest entered the Holy of Holies (God's presence) once a year in fear and trembling (Yom Kippur), today we can enter into God's presence at any time, with confidence, through the blood of Christ (Hebrews 10:19). Yet most believers rarely exercise this incredible privilege.

If we want to know God's will, we must ask Him for it. We will not discern it through simple human reasoning. As someone once said, "There is a lot you can do once you have prayed, but you can do nothing until you pray." If we run about trying to solve problems without first listening to God, we will be following ourselves like a dog chasing its own tail, and we will get nowhere.

The Promise of Prayer

In James 1:5 we find an incredible promise:

> If any of you lacks wisdom, let him ask of God, who gives to all men generously and without reproach, and it will be given to him.

God wants us to know His will, but He isn't going to force it on us. We must, in faith, ask Him for it, and when we do, He fulfills His promise.

One might well say that prayer is the ignition key to fire up the process of finding God's will. We cannot expect God to give us the wisdom we lack if we haven't even asked Him for it. Once we do, we can begin looking for His answer. But how does He reveal His answer? That is what the rest of this book details. Each of the remaining signposts reveals where to look for God's answers to the James 1:5 prayer. John Wesley put it this way:

> I find that the chief purpose of prayer in determining the will of God is to get my will in an unprejudiced state about the issue at hand. Then, when my will is unprejudiced, I find that God suggests reasons to my mind concerning the proper course.

The Practice of Prayer

It may seem a bit elementary to discuss the actual practice of prayer. I realize you may have cut your spiritual teeth on "Now I lay me down to sleep . . . " Prayer is simple, isn't it? Or is it? What I have observed in my ministry through the years is that most people perceive prayer as a ritual: kneeling and/or bowing the head, folding the hands, reciting a grocery list of requests interspersed with sixteenth-century English perhaps out of reverence for God or perhaps because we believe that is how God talks. Yet most of us really don't understand prayer as a fundamental part of a relationship with God.

Certain aspects of our faith are fundamental, things we never outgrow. We apply these things every day regardless of how mature we are in Christ. Prayer is one such fundamental. I am reminded of the great football coach, Vince Lombardi, who started the first practice of every season with the same line: "This is a football." His message was loud and clear — success isn't found in the flashy stuff, but in the fundamentals. The same is true in our spiritual lives.

The Fundamentals of Prayer

The first fundamental of prayer is that it is simply communicating with God from our hearts. Because of this, there is no such thing as an insincere prayer. If it isn't from our hearts, it isn't prayer, even if we call it that. It is only "lip-service." Like me, you have probably sat through prayer meetings where you wondered if any of the words even made it past the ceiling.

Unfortunately, many prayers offered in our prayer meetings are merely sermonettes to each other. Sadly, we worry so much about wording our prayer the right way that we forget we are talking to God. We fail to realize He isn't concerned about the wording as much as He is about our attitude. So the first fundamental of prayer is: *It must be honest communication from our heart to the heart of God.*

The second fundamental of prayer is that, contrary to the teachings of many, there is no power in prayer. Before you start tying me to the stake and piling up the brush, let me explain. Often we profess and promote the erroneous idea that prayer has some intrinsic power in itself. We place our faith in prayer instead of in God. This doctrine has its roots more in Eastern mysticism and the New Age movement than in biblical Christianity. True prayer is powerful only because God is powerful. *The real power of prayer is our connection with the all-powerful Creator God.* Prayer is not a means of twisting God's arm, but of communicating with Him openly.

The third fundamental of prayer is: *Nothing is off-limits.* We can (and should) pray about anything and everything. A great passage to educate us on the proper practice of prayer is Philippians 4:6,7: "Be anxious for nothing, but in everything by prayer and supplication with thanksgiving let your requests be made known to God." Here we find specific directions on how to proceed in prayer.

Directions for Prayer

First, we must *choose to lay aside our anxiety.* Anxiety should always be viewed as a red flag alerting us to the need to pray. Anxiety or worry can be a direct result of my trusting in myself and my own resources instead of in God. There are no guarantees that I will never be anxious, but if I let it dictate my response to God, it is sin, and it should be dealt with as such.

Next, the boundaries of prayer are given: *in everything.* No matter how much we weasel and squirm, we cannot escape the reality that God wants us to talk with

Him about everything, every area of our lives. Anything less is disobedience.

The third step in our process of prayer is *to pray.* This may sound silly, but the passage gives us specifics on how to go about this. First Paul says, "in everything by *prayer.*" This term just means general prayer directed to God. Next he says, "and *supplication.*" This term means to pray for particular benefits, in other words, to make our requests specific. Next, we are told to accompany these requests with *thanksgiving.* When we do all of these, we can make any request of God we desire, anything. Sound too good to be true? No, it is simply God's invitation to honesty. He wants us to bare our hearts to Him.

We must notice, however, that there is no promise God will give us our request. Sound unfair? Actually, what God promises is even better.

Instead of promising to honor our request, regardless of whether it is beneficial to us or not, God promises to guard our hearts with His peace. How does He do that? When we follow this very specific formula, we are, in essence, laying our request at God's feet. Once we've done that, we can have confidence that He hears us (Psalm 4:3). We can know that if our request is within His will, He'll give it to us. If not, He'll say no. Either way we can have peace because our request has now been filtered through God's will for us, which is good, acceptable, and perfect (Romans 12:1).

But what if God's will is not what I want? Ask yourself this: "Do I really want what my all-loving, all-knowing heavenly Father says is not the best for me?" Are you willing to settle for something less than God's will?

Barriers to Obeying This Sign

The biggest barriers to obeying the call to prayer are found in James 4:2 and 3: "You do not have because you do not ask. You ask and do not receive, because you ask with wrong motives." Let's break this passage down in light of what we already have talked about and see what it has to say.

We Do Not Ask

The first barrier James mentions is that we do not have because we do not ask. That had been my problem in the summer missions decision. Often, we simply try to figure out our own solutions instead of asking God for His. You may be saying, "But I have asked, and I still don't have." Let's analyze. In light of our fundamentals of true prayer, did your request really connect your faith to God, or did you place your faith in prayer? The difference is subtle but significant.

We Ask With Wrong Motives

A second barrier James mentions is that we do ask, but we ask with wrong motives. We don't really want God's will, we only want our own pleasure. This may be physical pleasure or it may be emotional pleasure — the pleasure of a trial-free, work-free existence. In any case, this wrong motive violates the necessary call to lordship we discussed in the last chapter. It is a commitment to our will instead of God's.

As I thought about the beach project my friend Mack had challenged me to, I ran into a lot of obstacles. *I am a really young Christian,* I thought. *What if I apply and don't get accepted?*

More pressing, though, was the fact that to apply would cost a ten-dollar non-refundable registration fee. For a guy working his way through college in the 1970s, that was a lot of money, more money than I had to spare. "Lord, if You want me to go on this summer missions project, You'll have to provide the ten dollars." That seemed an easy way to find the answer.

The next day was payday on my part-time job. I already had calculated the hours I had worked, and the check would be just barely enough to cover my bills and see me through to the next payday. Imagine my surprise when the check I picked up was over ten dollars more than what I had figured on. Turns out, my employer had made a mistake on a previous check and was making it up. "There's the ten dollars I prayed for!" I shouted to my roommate, as surprised that God answered my prayer as I was with how He did it.

I sent my application in and waited. I still wasn't fully convinced though. *After all this,* I thought, *what if I really don't get accepted?* So I did not turn down the camp job. On the summer project application they said they would let me know by April 10, and the camp director extended the final deadline for a decision until then. But April 10 came and I still hadn't heard from the summer project. "What should I do, Lord?" I prayed once again, frantically seeking an answer.

At that point, the Holy Spirit brought to mind what I had prayed the first time: "Lord, if you want me to go on this summer missions project, you'll have to provide the ten dollars." God had already given me my answer. I just had to take Him at His word and trust Him. Remember, James 1:6 says I must ask in faith. Even though I had no acceptance in hand, I did have God's leading, so I turned down the camp job. A few days later my summer project acceptance arrived, and that summer changed my life. It was the most intense time of spiritual growth I had experienced. It was one of many ways the Lord has shown me and reminded me that His will *is* good, acceptable, and perfect.

□□□

Putting It Into Practice

So where do we go from here? Let's review. We identified some specific steps to follow in praying for God's will as found in Philippians 4:6 and 7:

1. I must choose to lay aside my anxiety. I must transfer my trust from myself to God.
2. I must openly discuss every area with God.
3. I must direct my prayer to Him in a specific manner and accompany it with thanksgiving.
4. I may then bring *any* request to Him.
5. I must trust Him for His peace and accept His answer, whatever it is.

Prayer

Take a few minutes now to express your prayer in writing to the Lord in the space provided below:

5

Signpost #3

The TURN ON YOUR HEADLIGHTS Sign: Scripture

□□□□□

I just wish I knew what to do," Steve exclaimed with sincerity. Although he had been a believer for almost a year, he had been dating Susan since high school, and they were planning to get married as soon as they both finished college. It had never occurred to Steve that God might not approve of their relationship. Never, that is, until his pastor confronted him the week before. "Steve, you have to break up with her," he said. "She's not a Christian, and God would never bless that kind of marriage."

He had come away crushed. "I mean, it's not like we've been sleeping together or anything," he exclaimed. "Neither of us wants that until marriage. My dad says I should ignore him. He says the preacher is just legalistic. What do you think, Eddie?" he inquired.

Although I wasn't discipling Steve, we had often talked of our common faith in Christ, and it wasn't unusual for him to ask me questions about the Bible. This was different though. This wasn't some idle curiosity about Old Testament history or wondering where a certain verse was located. Steve was desperate for understanding and counsel, and he needed more of an answer than his pastor was giving him. He liked his church because of the friends he had made there, but often he questioned what the pastor taught, so I wasn't surprised Steve didn't jump at his advice.

"Do you think God won't bless our marriage just because Susan isn't a Christian?" Steve asked earnestly.

What would you say to Steve? Would you agree with the pastor and tell him God wouldn't bless his marriage to a non-Christian? Or would you tell him that as long as their relationship was morally okay, they could pursue it as far as they wanted? Or would you sweep the whole issue under the rug and say, "God will show you in time"? What would you say?

Steve needed more than simple opinions. He needed real answers, authoritative answers. Fortunately, God's will is not merely an issue of picking the opinion that sounds the best. God has given us His Word, which moves us from subjective opinions to objective authority. That is what this signpost is all about.

TURN ON YOUR HEADLIGHTS

As we continue on our road to God's will, we encounter a sign which reads TURN ON YOUR HEADLIGHTS. I remember as a child seeing such a sign at the entrance to one of my favorite road trip attractions: The Tunnel. Back in the days before Disney World and Darth Vader, that was big-time entertainment. And if we were really lucky, we'd experience the ultimate of thrills . . . Dad would honk the horn! I realize that isn't nearly so big a deal for my kids and possibly not for yours either, but perhaps like me, you have encountered a TURN ON YOUR HEADLIGHTS sign and found yourself wondering why people need to be reminded to do this. Truth is, dangerous as it is to drive in the dark without your headlights on, people still do it sometimes.

This principle applies to our spiritual lives as well. Psalm 119:105 tells us, "Thy Word is a lamp to my feet, and a light to my path."

God's Word is intended to illumine our way, yet so often in the midst of our need we forget to "turn on our headlights." Instead of going to God's Word for direction, we look elsewhere. God is light (1 John 1:5), and anything else, no matter how bright it appears, is darkness. What Steve needed was not the confusion of sorting through conflicting opinions, but the light and direction of God's Word.

The description of the working of God's Word we find in Psalm 119:105 pictures the spiritual truth of the illuminating work of Scripture. Consider the analogy. You are walking along a path at night with a lamp to show your way. The lamp doesn't illumine the path in its entirety. It merely creates a circle of light large enough to show you the next few steps on the path. It gives enough light to keep you from stumbling, but not so much that you are distracted from watching your step.

The Workings of God's Will

Not only does this analogy illustrate the working of God's Word, but it also gives clarity to understanding God's will. He doesn't reveal it in one big lump, but a little bit at a time. Paul Little, in his booklet *Affirming the Will of God* (InterVarsity, n.d.), expresses it this way:

> The will of God is not like a magic package let down from heaven by a string . . . the will of God is far more like a scroll that unrolls every day . . . the will of God is something to be discerned and lived out every day of our lives. It is not something to be grasped as a package once for all. Our call, therefore, is basically not to follow a plan or a blueprint, or to go to a place or take up a work, but rather to follow the Lord Jesus Christ.

One of the key ways we "follow the Lord Jesus Christ" is by living according to His Word. As Psalm 119:130 puts it: "The unfolding of Thy words gives light; it gives understanding to the simple." If you are like me, nothing makes you feel "simple" like trying to discern God's will. But, as Steve was about to find out, God's Word has the solution to that need.

Following God Through His Word

So how exactly do we follow God through His Word? To begin with, we must acknowledge one essential reality. Although you are probably grasping these principles of determining God's will in one specific area, it is imperative you realize that you will spend the rest of your Christian life seeking and finding the will of God. If our call is to follow Christ, then we will never outgrow our need to know His will. Because of this, let me suggest that the application really needs to be on two different levels.

First, like Steve, you probably have a present need to know God's will, and to meet it you will need to find Scriptures that address it. Some of these will be clear commands as to what the believer can and cannot do. Many of them, however, will give you principles that are to guide and direct you.

Because of this present need, you may want some help in finding these Scriptures. Two Bible tools will be helpful. An exhaustive concordance will help you find that verse you sort of remember but aren't sure where it is. The other resource is a topical Bible (such as *Nave's*). You probably can borrow this from your pastor or a friend, or pick one up at your local Christian bookstore. It will help you find passages involving the key topics you are considering. For example, if you are seeking God's will about marriage, it would be important to see what God's Word says about this subject.

Another resource in finding relevant passages will come from the counsel of godly Christians. We will take a thorough look at this resource in the next chapter.

As we seek to follow God through His Word, we will find answers to our immediate need, but since we will always be needing to find God's will, our present study of the Scriptures also lays a foundation for future insight.

David relates this in Psalm 37:31: "The law of his God is in his heart; his steps do not slip." The Word not only offers prescriptive answers for our present need, but works as preventive medicine for our future needs as well. This is what Paul had in mind in Romans 12:1 and 2 when he spoke of the transforming work of a "renewed" mind. He was referring to a mind that is deepening in the Word of God.

But what about areas where there is no "Thou shalt" or "Thou shalt not"? How do we determine God's will in the areas Scripture doesn't address? To begin with, let me emphasize that Scripture addresses life much more broadly than most people realize. Perhaps my counsel to Steve will help illustrate some of the many different ways God's Word speaks to our need.

"Steve, first of all, I don't want to just pile my opinion on top of everyone else's. I believe the Bible has a lot to say about this, and I think, instead of listening to me or anyone else, you ought to let the Scriptures tell you what to do." To start with, I directed him to Acts 17:11,12. "Here is a good attitude to have about Christian advice," I said as I showed him the Berean Christians' example:

Now these [the Bereans] were more noble minded than those in Thessalonica, for they received the Word with great eagerness, examining the Scriptures daily, to see whether these things were so. Many of them therefore believed.

Three important things set the Bereans apart. First, they were eager for the truth. They didn't just want their ears tickled and their preconceptions supported. Second, they checked out everything for themselves in the Bible. Too many Christians only know what their pastor tells them of the Bible. They never check it out for themselves. Finally, they were willing to act on what they learned.

"Now, Steve," I said, "the Bible can speak to us in four different ways, and I believe it uses all of them on this important issue of who to marry. Sometimes the Bible gives us clear commands, *proclamations* such as, 'Thou shalt' do something. Another way the Bible speaks to us is through *prohibitions*. This is when the Scripture says, 'Thou shalt not,' in a clear way. The third way Scripture speaks is through *promises*. Fourth, God's Word speaks to our need in the form of *principles*, wisdom from understanding how life is lived. Let me share some passages with you that speak in these ways."

Here is what I shared with Steve:

Principles

In Numbers 25 we can draw out some excellent principles on why it might not be wise to marry an unbeliever. It is the story of Balaam, a prophet of God who was hired to curse Israel. God wouldn't let him bring a curse on Israel, but because Balaam still wanted the pagan king's money, he apparently clued him in to how he could undermine Israel and lessen their threat: "Simply have your daughters intermarry with their sons and soon they will be no threat to you."

As Numbers 25 relates, it worked. Soon, instead of following God, Israel's sons followed their pagan wives into idol worship. In almost every biblical instance of believers marrying unbelievers, it is not the unbelieving spouse who is pulled up, but the believing spouse who is pulled down. (See Deuteronomy 7:1-4.)

Many other principles recorded in Scripture address this issue as well.

Promises

In Proverbs 31 we see some of the many blessings of being married to "a woman who fears the Lord." This positively affirms why it is worth it to wait for God to provide a believing wife. It relates the many joys you will be robbed of if you don't marry a believer.

Prohibitions

Perhaps the most familiar passage related on this subject is found in 2 Corinthians 6:14-18. Here the believer is very clearly admonished not to be unequally yoked with an unbeliever. A formal (legal) bond with an unbeliever, be it marriage or business partnership or whatever, is unacceptable to the Christian. The analogy here of being unequally yoked offers a graphic agricultural picture of the problems of such a relationship. Two undesirable results are described when a team of oxen are unequally yoked (a strong ox with a smaller, weaker one): Either the imbalance will cause the team to plow crooked, or the stronger ox will have to go slow since the weaker one is unable to keep pace.

Proclamations

Finally, Scripture also addresses this question in the form of a proclamation, a positive command. In 1 Corinthians 7:39 we learn that a widow, once her husband is dead, is free to marry whomever she wishes — with one restriction: "only in the Lord." She may remarry, but only a believer.

So where did this leave Steve? Although the Bible doesn't address every issue this thoroughly, the Scriptures had clearly shown from all angles that a believer marrying an unbeliever was not God's will. So he had his answer, right? Well maybe, and maybe not. You see, his question wasn't, "Can a Christian marry a non-Christian?" Rather, it was, "Is it okay for me to marry Susan?" As we conversed, I shared with him that very clearly he could not marry Susan, an unbeliever, and be following God's will, but that didn't mean Susan wouldn't come to share his faith in Christ. Steve didn't need an oversimplified answer and I wasn't going to give him one.

"Steve, here is my advice," I related. "First, realize that perhaps God has placed you in Susan's life so that she might hear and see the truth of God's love. Of all people, you should be the first to share with her about Christ. If I were you, I would take some time to explain to her how you came to know the Lord and what He means to you.

"Second, if she still isn't interested in spiritual things, something that is so important to you, then you have some hard choices to make. You're already 'unequally yoked' by dating her, and to continue in that relationship as it is will hinder your walk with Christ, not help it.

"Finally," I continued, "you need to be careful that you don't push Susan into an insincere commitment only to justify your marrying her. You need to make sure there is the evidence of her being a new creature in Christ before you go any further in this relationship. Remember, Steve, God's will for you is 'good, acceptable, and perfect.' If He doesn't want you to marry Susan, then His will is better. Don't shortchange yourself by settling for anything less than God's best."

As you can see from the above discussion, the Word of God speaks much more broadly to life than we sometimes think. Even if the Bible has no "Thou shalts" or "Thou shalt nots" to speak to our circumstances, there are principles that always relate.

God has not left us to make life's decisions in the dark. We have the light of His Word to illumine our feet and light our path.

Barriers to Obeying This Sign

As we look at the signposts of Scripture, it will help us if we consider some of the road blocks that hinder our obedience to these principles. The clear leading of God by itself doesn't guarantee the believer will be on the right track. We must accurately interpret God's leading, and we must choose to follow it. There are several potential barriers to our obeying this sign.

The most significant barrier to our obedience is the danger of *mishandling God's Word.* Paul exhorted his disciple, the young pastor Timothy, "Be diligent to present yourself approved to God as a workman who does not need to be ashamed, handling accurately the word of truth" (2 Timothy 2:15). If we are not careful, our desire for God's will to be a particular thing may subtly corrupt the interpretation process, and we may read our own ideas into the Scriptures.

Not long ago I was looking back through an old journal from my college days and was reminded of this principle. At the time I was dating a young lady and really wanted the relationship to lead to marriage. As I read the Bible, I had found some Scriptures that seemed to support my desire and began to build my hope around them. I used these verses to convince myself that she was my future mate. Later, when God led me to break up with her and made it clear she was not to be my wife, I saw that I had read into those Scriptures what I wanted to see. I had not interpreted them in the light of their context, but in light of my desires.

I learned the hard way that God does not speak to us from His Word like a Ouija board. An interpretation that discounts and violates a verse's meaning in its context is a wrong interpretation. This is not "handling accurately the word of truth."

Another danger in applying this principle is *not getting a balanced view of Scripture.* No one verse or passage stands by itself, but each must be interpreted in light of the whole. Again, the counsel of others will help guard against error.

It almost goes without saying, but a final way we can miss the boat is that once we discern what God's Word is saying, we still *must make that choice to obey.* Steve had direction, but he still had to choose to follow it. Fortunately, God's Word helps us at this point as well. In Psalm 40:8 King David shares an important truth: "I delight to do Thy will, O my God; Thy Law is within my heart." In other words, not only does Scripture show us what God wants us to do, but being in the Word also creates in us a desire to obey what He says.

❑❑❑

Applications

1. What issues related to my situation has God already spoken about in His Word?

2. What are some relevant passages* and their
   messages to my situation?

   Passage #1:

   Its message:

   Passage #2:

   Its message:

   Passage #3:

   Its message:

   Passage #4:

   Its message:

*NOTE: If you are unable to locate adequate passages of
Scripture at this point, don't worry. More will surface
through counsel with others, and you can come back
and include these as they do.

6

Signpost #4

The INFORMATION Sign:
Counsel

□□□□□

Rich breathed a sigh of relief as he wrote out his resignation. He had hated his job from day one, but the money had been good, and with a baby on the way they would soon be losing his wife's income. Rich had initially thought he could do the job even though he knew it wasn't the sort of work he enjoyed. But after three months of always being tired and grouchy, of always dreading to go to work, of hating the demands his boss made on him, Rich had had enough. No job, he reasoned, was worth what he was going through, no matter how bad they needed the money. Besides, he had an idea.

Rich had always enjoyed building things. In fact, the country-style woodworking items he made in his basement were very popular among their friends. More than one of them said he could earn a living with such fine woodcrafting. "Barbra, I'm going to do it!" he exclaimed with enthusiasm as he shared his idea with his wife. "I'm quitting my job and I'm going to start a woodworking business in the basement. I can be my own boss and work my own hours and I'll even be home to watch the baby when you need to go out!"

Like water on a wood fire, the look on Barbra's face dampened his enthusiasm. Even before she exploded in anger that turned to tears, he knew her enough to read the fearful look in her eyes. When the emotions subsided, they talked long and hard about Rich's idea. Barbra knew the factory job had been tough on him. "But what if your idea doesn't work?" she pleaded. "How will we get by with me not working? How will we pay the mortgage? Would you talk with elder Robins first . . . before you do anything?" she asked.

Rich was confused. He had been so confident this was the answer to their problems, but now he wasn't so sure. "What should I do, Lord?" he entreated silently as he laid his resignation aside.

INFORMATION

The next signpost we encounter on the road to God's will is the INFORMATION sign. It is divinely designed to remind us that we don't always know all the answers, and sometimes we need to ask directions. I am notorious for getting lost when I take my family on vacation trips — and I hesitate to stop and ask directions. Maybe you can relate. Most of us either have done it or have ridden in a car with a like-minded driver. It takes so little time to stop and ask directions but pride keeps prodding us to try to figure it out on our own.

Unfortunately, this same phenomenon shows itself in our spiritual lives. Often as we seek to find God's will we fail to draw upon the maturity and wisdom of our friends in the body of Christ. Yet clearly God desires that we do this. That doesn't mean every time we don't know what to do we drop the burden in someone else's lap; nor does it mean we should seek counsel from a professional. Any Christian who is mature and knows the Word of God should be able to counsel other believers he knows. What we are talking about here is advice, and that was what Rich needed before making such an important decision.

How Counsel Can Help

One way counsel can benefit us is to help us find objectivity. When we are in the middle of a circumstance and are trying to discern God's will, it is often hard to be objective. Our emotions and desires can flavor even our most sincere efforts. Someone who isn't wrapped up in the process or bound by its consequences can look at things more easily and with objectivity. Rich needed to realize that his desire to leave a bad working situation could cloud his objectivity and move him to a decision he might later regret. Proverbs 12:15 tells us, "The way of a fool is right in his own eyes, but a wise man is he who listens to counsel." In other words, we need to recognize our ability to deceive ourselves and be willing to listen to those around us.

Another way advice can help us to find God's will is through shared wisdom, insight and experience. One person cannot hope to be adequately informed on everything. So it is essential that we pool our resources with those around us. Proverbs 15:22 puts it this way: "Without consultation, plans are frustrated, but with many counselors they succeed."

No believer, regardless of maturity, is immune to this need for occasional counsel. We do not have to look far in the Scriptures to see the principle illustrated. In 2 Samuel 24 we read of David's sinful decision to take a census of the people. The implied purpose was to see how big an army he could put together for battle, indicating his trust in numbers rather than in God. Joab, the commander of the army, counseled David against the move but David did not listen, nor did he seek counsel elsewhere.

The consequences of David's lack of consultation were great. Although God had provided His guidance and the knowledge of His will through the counsel He placed around David, David's refusal to listen made him susceptible to error. As a result, 70,000 men died in the ensuing plague.

Even though David was a mature believer, a man after God's own heart, he was still capable of mistakes in judgment. Each of us shares that same potential. That is why God places us in a body with relationships of accountability and encouragement.

A Parallel Principle

A principle that parallels this concept of counsel is found in the Jewish legal system. Our American legal idea of "innocent until proven guilty" is based largely on the Jewish legal guidelines which state: "By the mouth of two or three witnesses every fact may be confirmed" (Deuteronomy 19:15; Matthew 18:16). In other words, a person is innocent until an allegation is confirmed by two or more independent witnesses. This guards against false accusations.

So how does this relate to God's will? It is my conviction that we should not base a conclusion about God's will or leading from only one area. Although God does give us leading through His peace, because of the danger of misinterpretation it is unwise to draw a conclusion based only on God's peace. The same holds true for any of the signposts to God's will. To guard against false leading, we need to apply the principle of "two or three witnesses," and we should wait for God to begin lining up signposts so as not to draw a conclusion from only one source.

The wise thing for Rich to do was to seek counsel, and even more, to listen to the counsel he had already received from his wife. Even though I don't always listen to her as quickly as I should, I have learned that God often speaks wisdom to me through my wife. Even when I don't follow her advice, I benefit by taking the time to understand what she is saying.

The Criteria for Counselors

How do I find good counsel? Who should I go to? What criteria do I use? Finding good counsel involves many factors, and it is important that before you talk to people, you decide whom you want to listen to. Here is a list of criteria I use in varying degrees. They are not listed in order of priority or of value.

1. Spiritual maturity

2. Personal maturity and wisdom

3. Commitment to the will of God

4. Someone who knows you well (knows your strengths and weaknesses)

5. Your family elders (parents, grandparents, etc.)

6. Someone familiar with your particular situation

7. Someone familiar with your type of situation (e.g., for marriage counsel look to someone who does that type of counseling)

8. Someone who can be objective, who has nothing to gain or lose by your decision (someone who will get the commission from the sale is not the best counsel in buying a car)

9. People you respect and are willing to listen to (a non-negotiable)

I don't necessarily look for people who fit all the above categories perfectly, but rather, for different people who fit a few of them exceptionally well. For example, one counselor might know me very well and have a good degree of personal maturity but may not be as spiritually minded as others. That person could offer valuable input. Another might have great spiritual depth but not know me as well. The key is balance. Don't make all your counselors fit the same mold.

Barriers to Obeying This Sign

As with each of the signposts we are considering, there is the potential of misinterpretation. The most common methods of mistake in this area are (a) selecting the wrong counselors; (b) not listening to them; and (c) leaning more on human counsel than on what God has to say.

First, realize that the counsel is only as good as the counselors. That is why it is essential that you determine criteria for whom you are going to listen to. One common danger is *our tendency to seek counselors who will tell us what we want to hear.* I've found that often my critics make good counselors if they can listen without taking it personally. They help me see a side I don't naturally see. Be sure the person you select is suited to advise in your situation. A single person may not have as much wisdom to offer in a marriage decision as someone who is married. Be choosy in picking your advisors.

The second danger is *not listening to the counsel we receive.* Don't bother going through the process if you aren't willing to let God speak to you through others. Often we don't mind hearing what others think, but in our heart we've already decided what we want to do.

A third danger is *letting the majority rule.* This may be the American way, but it isn't God's way. A classic example is the men who spied out Canaan. The majority said don't go in and the people listened to them, but it was the minority (Joshua and Caleb) who had God's heart.

The church I presently minister with is ruled by a counsel of elders, and major decisions require a unanimous vote. On several occasions I have been held in check by the reservations of one elder only later to be glad I did not proceed.

The final potential problem with this signpost is that we may tend to *lean more on human counsel than on God.* As with each signpost, don't make this one principle stand by itself. Listen to counsel but, most important, listen to God. Sometimes what God says is the opposite of what the counselor says. The key issue with counsel is not just listening to it, but also hearing what God might be saying through that counselor.

I remember some advice given me by one well-meaning pastor a number of years ago. I was attempting to plant a new ministry on a largely commuter campus near our ministry base, and I was having my doubts. It was a tough place to build a ministry. Most of the students lived at home and had part-time jobs. In a meeting with some key pastors in the town to see what could be done, one chided, "That campus chews up Christian workers and spits them out every year. What makes you think you'll be able to plant a ministry there?"

Rather than dissuading me as it was intended to, his message became a motivator to me. It was as if the Lord were saying, "Eddie, when the ministry is built, I can get all the glory," and I was reminded that "nothing will be impossible with God" (Luke 1:37). Now, some years later, when I am invited to speak at this Christian gathering, I find it continuing to thrive as it reaches people for Christ. I remember that pastor's words and I marvel at the greatness of my God.

"Mr. Robins, as a businessman what do you think about my idea?" Rich asked. It was a few days later, and he had acted on Barbra's advice. He met with Bill Robins, one of the elders at their church and a very successful business entrepreneur.

"Well, Rich," Mr. Robins confided, "it sounds to me like your idea has a lot of potential, but you need to realize the odds are stacked against you. Most new businesses don't make it.

"You see, just having a good product is no guarantee of success in the business world. You have to drum up sales, keep your overhead down through wise purchases and good business decisions, and know when to expand

and how. Building a successful business that can support you is a complicated task.

"My advice to you," Mr. Robins concluded, "is, don't quit your job until your business begins to show that it can make it. Work at it on the side as long as you can. As your business grows, you'll be able to pick up the business sense to keep it going without the risk of losing your shirt and letting down your family. Businesses that take the time to build up some capital and develop their clientele before trying to carry the burden of supporting you are a lot more likely to make it. Yet even if it never develops to a point of supporting you, at least it should give you a good supplemental income."

In the lean months ahead as Rich built his business, he was glad he waited a while before quitting his job.

◻◻◻

Application Notes

Take a look at the criteria I listed for counselors and begin thinking of who you can look to for advice. Once you have selected your counsel, record their directions in the space provided.

COUNSEL #1:

COUNSEL#2:

COUNSEL#3:

COUNSEL#4:

7

Signpost #5

The WEIGH STATION *Sign:* Counting The Cost

□□□□□

othing is quite so unnerving as the unexpected scream of a 5-year-old from directly behind your head after you have been driving for three hours. Our toddler was reaching in both directions from his car seat in the middle of our back seat and was pulling both his brother's and his sister's hair. I was tempted to pull out mine. Somewhere along about the thirteenth time this happened, my resolve weakened and I agreed with my wife that it was time to get a larger car. The compact station wagon had served us well and had been a dependable car through the past six years and 100,000 plus miles. However, this family of five definitely needed to catch up with the times, and we began looking at the possibility of buying a used minivan.

"Which one should we buy?" became a frequent topic of discussion at the Rasnake household.

As I delved into the decision-making process, I quickly learned that buying a car involves more than just a simple choice. It is a myriad of little choices. What color? What size? Do we want a luggage rack? Power windows? Power locks? Cruise control? Sun roof? Do we want a cassette player or just an AM/FM radio? Vinyl or carpeted floor mats? Is undercoat rust protection important? Do we want an extended warrant? Do we pocket the rebate, or get 2.9-percent financing from the dealer, or do we go to the bank and borrow the money? How does our faith in Christ help us handle this?

You may wonder what all this has to do with God's will, or if I really believe God cares if we get a red Chrysler or a blue Ford. The truth is, many Christians make a big mistake when they divorce such decisions from the wisdom God has to offer. No, God will not write in the sky: "Buy the blue one, and don't forget cruise control." However, He has given some principles in Scripture that help us in managing the finances He provides.

WEIGH STATION

The next signpost we encounter on the road to God's will is the WEIGH STATION sign. Often, as we travel on our highways, we see trucks lined up at these stations to weigh in. This sign reminds us of the need to weigh our options carefully as we make decisions. We must count the cost ahead of time. To make a good decision, we need to do some homework. We need to find out as much as we can about every aspect of the choice to be made. To a degree, our final decision is only as good as the information we base it on.

Jesus emphasized this principle in Luke 14 as He explained His challenging statement, "Whoever does not carry his own cross and come after Me cannot be My disciple" (verse 27). To illustrate, Jesus related two hypothetical situations.

The Principle Illustrated

First, Jesus said,

Which one of you, when he wants to build a tower, does not first sit down and calculate the cost, to see if he has enough to complete it? Otherwise, when he has laid a foundation, and is not able to finish, all who observe it begin to ridicule him, saying, "This man began to build and was not able to finish" (Luke 14:28-30).

This story creates a graphic mental picture of the necessity of counting the cost. In my mind I can visualize a half-built tower with weeds growing up in the center. The mortar is crumbling in places and stones lay scattered on the ground. Strangers gawk as they pass by and neighbors share a knowing smirk as they look at it, a monument to not counting the cost. I know what that feels like all too well. Our last car was a good one, but soon after I bought it, I learned I could have gotten the same car with the same features for about $1,500 less. I thought about that every month when I made the payment, and that fact motivates me to do my homework.

As if for double emphasis, Jesus related a second illustration:

> Or what king, when he sets out to meet another king
> in battle, will not first sit down and take counsel
> whether he is strong enough with ten thousand men
> to encounter the one coming against him with twenty
> thousand? Or else, while the other is still far away,
> he sends a delegation and asks for terms of peace
> (Luke 14:31,32).

It may very well be that Christ drew both of these hypothetical illustrations from Proverbs 20:18: "Prepare plans by consultation, and make war by wise guidance." Getting advice and counsel from others, as discussed in the last chapter, is a significant factor in counting the cost.

One might argue that this isn't really a separate signpost but is the application of all of them. I chose to separate it for two reasons: (1) for emphasis; and (2) because it teaches us that different questions sometimes require different types of answers.

With the first illustration, the building of a tower, Jesus shows how our principle applies in a whether-to-or-not decision. In the second, He builds on that idea pointing to an either-or decision. In the first, it would be okay if no decision were made. The project would simply remain on hold. With the second, however, some decision had to be made. The implication is that the king realized, after counting the cost, that fighting might be futile, so he pursued an alternative: to seek acceptable peace terms.

I like the second illustration. It shows the process of counting the cost. David becomes an example — he tried to determine the strength of his army. Reading between the lines, it would seem he was not only identifying their numerical strength but also their valor. He asks himself, "Are my ten thousand valiant enough to tackle his twenty thousand?" Notice there is no answer, no indication of a decision. Perhaps it is too close to call, so he investigates his other options. He sends a delegation to the approaching king to see what the terms of surrender would be. Notice the time factor, too. He sends his inquiry "while the other is still far away." He doesn't wait until the last minute.

We can learn much about counting the cost from these words of Christ. Applying some of these principles to buying a vehicle meant going to the library and reading up on safety records and consumer reports. It meant praying over our family budget to see what we could afford and how that would affect our freedom to give to the Lord's work. It meant test drives and shopping around. Homework isn't always easy, but neither is living with the consequences of an unwise choice.

Certainly, we would consider someone foolish who undertook a building project without first determining if he could afford to finish it. Likewise, we would have little sympathy for a king who goes to war without adequate forethought. Yet so often we fail to apply this principle in areas of our own life. We make purchases that blow our budget. We say yes to projects we don't have time for. We make spur-of-the-moment decisions we later regret. None of us is immune from error. What is required is cultivating the habit of counting the cost.

Identifying the Need

The process of counting the cost involves several steps. As we look at Christ's message in Luke 14:27-30, we can identify many of them. In both of His illustrations we see that the first step in counting the cost is to identify the needs presented. In the case of the tower, the builder must "sit down and calculate the cost." Alfred Plummer, in his *Critical and Exegetical Commentary on the Gospel*

According to St. Luke (Fortress, 1901), points out that the phrase "sit down" represents "long and serious consideration," not just idle thought. Of course this consideration would apply to the finances, estimating how much the materials and hired manpower would cost. It would also apply to time: how much time he would have to put in personally, and how long the project would take.

The king going into battle would have to determine the size and strength of the opposition. How many soldiers do they have? How many horses or camels will they bring?

Do you see the principle? The first step we undertake should be to understand the need clearly.

Understanding the Resources

As we study Christ's explanation, the next step we see is to identify and inventory the relevant resources at our disposal. For the man building a tower, the resources would be his finances, his servants and workers, and his raw materials. How much money could he afford to spend? How many presently on his payroll could he involve in the task, and how many could he hire? How much of the needed materials (trees, stone, etc.) does he already have?

For the king going into battle, the resources would be the manpower and military equipment available to him. His determination would need to be both qualitative and quantitative.

Factoring in Time

The example of the king going into battle presents us with two additional principles: (1) factoring in time; and, (2) evaluating other options. The king, in a timely manner, might determine what the other army expected for a peace treaty.

To factor in time, our third principle, requires adequate forethought. Don't wait to start making a decision until it has to be made. Doing this opens us up to hasty, sometimes unwise, decisions without being able to count the cost. We must plan to plan. We must begin gathering information and evaluating it before the deadline.

In college I was notorious for putting off writing papers until the last minute. I had convinced myself that the pressure helped me. In reality, however, I often found myself writing without time to do adequate research and with my senses dulled by all-nighters at the typewriter. It took some time for me to realize that the grades I got on such projects didn't adequately reflect my abilities. I was settling for less because I was too lazy to plan ahead. Don't we often do the same thing in decision making? Don't we sometimes settle for less than the best because we don't factor in time?

Our king allowed himself adequate time to calculate by starting early. He also may have bought himself some time by negotiating. By sending a delegation to meet the opposing army, he stalled them. He persuaded them to wait for the process. If our king still decided to fight, he had bought precious time to prepare his defenses. You can fight a defensive battle with fewer men if you prepare properly.

So what does this say to us about practicality?

First, we can factor in time by beginning early, not waiting till the deadline. Second, we can factor in time by involving the one with the deadline in our information-gathering process. We don't do this simply as a stall tactic but to make sure we can adequately count the cost.

Evaluating Other Options

An additional lesson we can learn from our king is to evaluate our other options. As we shared in the earlier chapter on "The Binary Trap," rarely do situations present us with only two options. If nothing else, time (waiting) is always a third. Our king, rather than limiting himself to either winning or losing the battle, began checking to see if he could come up with some other option. He inquired of the other king as to his terms for peace.

Often in biblical times, such a peace treaty would involve slavery as well as forfeiture of lands and goods. There is no indication in Christ's example, but we can infer from His scenario that the king would then have to sit down and evaluate the terms for peace to see if they were worth accepting, or if instead he would take his troops into battle and pray for God to intervene on their behalf. In some cases a fight to the death would be better than surrender. Some nations would torture them and rape their women. In such a case, the king had much to evaluate, and he would need to do whatever he could to increase his options.

If we desire to make effective decisions, we often will need to create our own options rather than limit ourselves to only those presented to us. Daniel and his three friends did that. The Babylonian authorities placed them in a binary situation. They gave them only two options: either eat from the king's menu and violate God's dietary restrictions, or refuse and face the king's wrath. I'm sure Daniel evaluated the situation and said to himself, "I don't like either choice," so he became creative. He took it upon himself to come up with an alternative that satisfied both camps. Daniel realized the king's goal wasn't really to make him eat the food but to make him as healthy as possible, so he suggested a test to show that God's diet plan would reach that goal better. In the end, everyone came out a winner. That is a worthy goal in negotiation: Try to find a way for everyone to win.

Barriers to Obeying This Sign

As with each of our signposts, the potential of misapplication or non-application applies. To avoid this mistake we must consider the dangers. The WEIGH STATION sign does us no good if we don't stop at it, but even when we do, we can be misled in several ways.

One potential danger is that *counting the cost becomes an excuse for deferring a decision.* We use it to avoid making a final decision. Some of us have a difficult time finalizing a decision. We vacillate and second-guess ourselves silly. If this is true of you, part of the problem may be simply inexperience and a lack of education in biblical decision-making. But it also may be rooted in personality and background.

If you grew up in a family where all your decisions were critiqued by your parents and frequently found wanting by their standards, you may have difficulty trusting your own decisions as an adult. If you tend to be a perfectionist, you may spend too much time counting the cost and trying to come up with a perfect decision. One of the realities of decision-making is that more often than not, we don't have as much information as we want, but the decision still has to be made. Change in these areas will be slow, but becoming aware of weaknesses is a step in the right direction.

One danger we need to be mindful of is *making decisions by default.* I saw this many times in my years of ministry with college students. Often, students would not take advantage of an opportunity, such as a conference or a retreat, not because they sought the Lord and decided not to go, but because they put off deciding until it was too late to go. They decided by not deciding—a negative decision by default. I see the same tendencies in some of the adults I minister to now. Realize this: It is okay and biblically right sometimes to decide to wait, but it is wrong and it is sin to decide by not making a decision.

Another danger when we apply this principle of counting the cost is leaning too heavily on it. The **WEIGH STATION** principle fosters a danger of *making decisions by sight, not faith.* Finances play a role in some decisions, but sometimes even when the finances aren't there, God leads us to do something and He wants us to trust Him to provide the finances. The same is true of many other aspects of counting-the-cost decisions. Even when we have counted the cost, we must be willing to make a faith decision, not simply a sight one.

When Gideon marched with his army of three hundred, a sight decision would have sent him home instead of into battle. When Moses and Israel had Pharaoh at their backs and the Red Sea in front of them, a sight decision would have said surrender instead of sending them through the sea. We must count the cost, but our calculating scales must make room for God.

I remember my first year of full-time ministry with college students at the University of Virginia. After one semester, I was convinced that the attitudes of the high academic and upper-middle-class students and the restrictions of the administration made a movement of impact for Christ unlikely, if not impossible. But God brought me to the point where I realized no matter how many reasons it wouldn't work that I could fit on one side of the scale, God was still on the other. Years later, the men God allowed me to invest my life in there are still serving Christ all over the globe. We do need to count the cost, but God must be included in our counting.

Applying this WEIGH STATION principle proved very helpful for me in buying a vehicle. Shopping around, I discovered that buying hubcaps, floormats, and a stereo from Kmart instead of the dealer would save me several hundred dollars. *Consumer Report* magazine taught me that much hidden profit for a car dealer is built into exorbitant mark-up prices for inexpensive services such as underbody rust protection and stain-guard treatment for fabric seats. Simple addition and subtraction showed me that discount interest rates from dealers really wouldn't save me money, especially if it meant buying a different car from the one I wanted.

□□□

Applying the Principle

What about you? Have you done your homework on the decision you need to make? "Better safe than sorry" and "An ounce of prevention is worth a pound of cure" became clichés because they are true. Use the following structured questions to assist you in counting the cost of your decision:

Identify the Need. In the space below, clarify as near as you can the need or circumstances confronting you.

Identify Your Resources. List as completely as you can the resources you have that bear on this decision.

Factor in Time. How much time do you have to make this decision?

What do you need to do to insure that you have enough time to do a good job?

Options. What are your present options in this decision?

How can you modify these to make them better suited?

What options can you create to resolve the situation better?

8

Signpost #6

The DETOUR *Sign:*
Providential
Circumstances

□□□□□

E ddie, I really believe you are the man for the job."
These words, coming from an old friend and former pastor, were like music to my ears. I was in
the middle of the lengthy and sometimes frustrating process of interviewing for the job of youth pastor at the
Baptist church I had first attended as a new believer, and
it was reassuring to hear again that the pastor both wanted
me for the job and believed I would get it.

During college I had gotten a clear sense from the
Lord of a calling into the ministry, but I wasn't certain

when or where. Upon graduation I took a job managing a restaurant. The money was good, especially now that I was engaged and soon to have a wife to support. But the hours were long and the chances to minister were few and far between. From inside I sensed a deepening longing to give the Lord the best hours of my day in service, not just the leftovers.

When I had heard that my former church was looking for a youth pastor, my heart skipped a beat. God had greatly used the saintly pastor to ground me in the faith. He taught the Scriptures well and had a strong sense of burden for the lost. The thought of working alongside him and learning from him seemed too good to be true, but after I met with him, we both knew we wanted it to work out. Now I was going through the interview process with the search committee and was patiently biting my nails as they interviewed others. Not only would this job allow me to get into the ministry full-time, but it would also mean a better salary, good news for the potential newlyweds.

The church that was interviewing me had started with a list of fifteen potential candidates, which quickly narrowed to ten. The pastor frankly shared with me that he considered me at the top of the list. The group was narrowed to five and then to three, and he still believed I was the man for the job. I knew I wanted it more now than ever. Finally the list was narrowed to two men, myself and another, and the pastor affirmed his belief in me.

The committee however was divided. They had committed to make a unanimous decision, but they could not seem to come to agreement. The process had gone on for more than six months and a decision had to be made so a deadline was set.

I was nervous with excitement as I dialed the phone to find out their decision from the pastor. My wedding was a month away and my wife and I had found an apartment. In fact, we had already started planning our budget based on the new salary. As soon as the pastor answered I knew something was wrong. He said, "Eddie, I would never have believed what happened tonight," and he began to explain what I already sensed.

The committee had been deadlocked. Some wanted me for the job, others wanted the other fellow, and none were willing to budge. After hours of deliberation, there seemed no way to come to agreement. Then someone remembered a Bible verse about Judas' replacement being chosen by casting lots. Quickly everyone agreed to the plan and both names were placed into a hat as they prayed for God to use this to direct them. "Eddie, I really believed your name was going to come out of the hat," the pastor painfully related.

Suddenly my world had shattered.

DETOUR

Perhaps tougher to accept, but no less valid, one of the important signposts we come to on the road to God's will is the DETOUR sign. I encountered a DETOUR sign the other day when I was out driving. At first I thought it was an annoying inconvenience. But when I discovered it had been placed there because of a washed-out bridge, I recognized it served for my protection. I wonder how many times life's detour signs, though frustrating and inconvenient, have served through God's sovereignty to protect me. God speaks through our circumstances, and we can save ourselves much anxiety if we learn to listen to what they say. Are there some DETOUR signs in your life?

The Divine Design of Detours

What did I learn from my experience? I saw two clear purposes behind God's sovereign working: (1) He wants to *provide* for me; and, (2) He wants to *protect* me. His will provides the best of everything. There is no wasted time in it. And His will protects me from anything counter to His design. When His will has so much to offer, it makes no sense to settle for mine. Often, in His gracious sovereignty, He places a detour on my path to put me back on His. Getting turned down for the youth-pastor job did that for me.

You see, during my last year of college I sensed the Lord leading me to join the staff of Campus Crusade for Christ to have a ministry reaching college students for Him. I said yes, went through the application process, and was accepted on staff. As my time to go through training and begin raising my support neared, I began having second thoughts. "I just didn't have a peace about it," I explained to friends. Truth is, I was fearful of trusting God to raise my support. I wasn't looking forward to months of asking people I didn't know to invest in my ministry.

So when I was offered a restaurant management job, I jumped at the chance for a steady salary, and thus began eighteen months of unhappiness. The story of Jonah graphically illustrates that no one is more miserable than the person running from God's call. Like what the huge fish did for Jonah, a DETOUR sign put me back on the path of God's leading.

We see this principle operating in the life of the apostle Paul many times. In his letter to the believers at Philippi, he addressed their concern over his "detour" to prison, and points them to a different perspective:

> Now I want you to know, brethren, that my circumstances have turned out for the greater progress of the gospel, so that my imprisonment in the cause of Christ has become well known throughout the whole praetorian guard [about 9,000 men] and to everyone else, and that most of the brethren, trusting in the Lord because of my imprisonment, have far more courage to speak the word of God without fear (Philippians 1:12-14).

God's detour provided greater evangelism opportunities for Paul as well as greater faith and boldness for the Roman church. It also protected him from the deadly intentions of antagonistic Jews whose plot to kill him was thwarted by his arrest.

Another detour sign in the Scriptures is seen in the scattering of the early church. Christ's last command to the church at His ascension was to take the gospel to the "remotest part of the earth" (Acts 1:8), yet it wasn't until the persecution that began with Stephen that believers began to leave Jerusalem. The persecution served as a catalyst to spread the gospel to the world by spreading believers throughout the world. Because God is sovereign, Satan's attempt to stamp out Christianity turned out for the progress of the gospel, a divinely designed detour: God took what men meant for evil and used it for good.

What Detours Look Like

God's detours take many different shapes and sizes. Sometimes, as in Paul's experience in Ephesus (1 Corinthians 16:8,9), God speaks to us through "open doors," divinely designed opportunities for ministry. Other times, as in Paul's efforts to take the gospel to Asia and Bithynia (Acts 16:6,7), He speaks through closed doors. Although my initial choice not to join the staff because of support raising reflected some weakness of faith, I still wanted to do God's will. The detour sign of not getting the church job put me back on the previous path. Six months later, I did follow the Lord's leading and joined the Campus Crusade staff. It is important to realize that every open door does not constitute a call, and every closed door doesn't mean we give up, but God can and sometimes does speak through such circumstances.

The main point of the detour sign is that God, in His sovereignty, may give us detours to get us on the right road. When you think about it, this is truly an encouraging thought. Because God desires even more than we do that we be in His will, He is willing and able to redirect us if we sincerely want to follow Him. Have you ever experienced that? I have.

Barriers to Obeying This Sign

As with each of the signposts to God's will, there is the potential of misapplication. If we aren't careful, we might draw the wrong conclusions about what God is saying. As we noted above, *an open door or opportunity doesn't automatically mean God is the one calling.*

Satan also places open doors in our path. When he tempted Jesus in the wilderness, he presented Him with the opportunity to have "all the kingdoms of the world" (see Matthew 4:8).

Sometimes, too, other pressing needs come before an open door. We see this in Paul's second letter to

Corinth. He had an open door for ministry in Troas, but the Lord led him to pass it up and go to Macedonia to see how the Corinthians were doing (2 Corinthians 2:12,13).

So how do we know when an open door is God's will? I think the important principle to recognize here is that an open door must be considered carefully. It is God's will that we go to Him about open doors and not dismiss them without prayer. When I am faced with an open door, I seek the Lord about it, and I trust Him to confirm His will with several signposts. No one signpost is confirmation by itself.

Another ever-present danger in looking at our circumstances is that *we might interpret them by our feelings instead of by faith.* A troubling question came from my church job experience: How could I be so sure something was God's will and be so wrong? Perhaps you have made similar misjudgments. We all need to recognize how easily personal desires can get in the way of understanding clearly what God is saying. My longing to be in the ministry and my love for my former pastor had clouded my interpretation of God's leading. Circumstances can be misinterpreted easily, and our human wants or our fleshly desire for comfort may deceive us into seeing something as God's will when it isn't.

Let's face it. No one likes trials. Nobody wants to go through difficult circumstances. I don't particularly like the idea that persecution might be God's will for me. I'd rather stick my head in the sand and naïvely believe that life is supposed to be easy. However, God is far more concerned with my character than with my circumstances. In fact, circumstances are one of His favorite tools to shape my character. He would like me to learn my lessons academically through studying the Word, but He also lets me learn them vocationally by putting me into situations where I have to apply what the Word says.

If we aren't careful, we will mistake our fleshly desire for ease and comfort for God's leading. It isn't surprising that people buy into wrong doctrines — those teaching that, if we'll just have enough faith, we'll have all the money we want, all the healing we want, everything. We really want those things to be true, but God doesn't fit neatly into our box, and often His use of providential circumstances means difficult times for us.

There is good news in this, though. Because God is sovereign, He is able to turn the difficult times around and cause them to work for our good. Notice I am not saying that God causes bad things to happen to His people. What I am saying is that, because He is sovereign, He can use anything that happens to us to accomplish His will. And when I grumble and complain about my circumstances, in effect, I am accusing God of mismanaging my life.

Sovereignty and Circumstance

Consider the story of Joseph, Jacob's son. His jealous brothers sold him into slavery, and then his master's wife wrongly accused him of attempted rape and he was thrown into prison.

Where was God in all of this? Right in the middle. God used these difficult, painful detours to accomplish His will. He turned them around and used Joseph's slavery and prison experience to place him as Prime Minister over all of Egypt. Now that is what I call sovereignty!

Notice what Joseph learns in all of this. When his brothers come to him fearing he would have them killed, he replied:

Do not be afraid, for am I in God's place? And as
for you, you meant evil against me, but God meant
it for good in order to bring about this present result
(Genesis 50:19,20).

This is a classic example of what Romans 8:28 tells us:

We know that God causes all things to work together
for good to those who love God, to those who are
called according to His purpose.

Because God is sovereign, He is able to accomplish
His purpose through whatever life throws at us, and He
does. He "causes *all* things" to work toward His ultimate
purpose. What an incredible principle!

So how do I respond to the difficult circumstances
that come my way? Do I just passively assume they are
God's will and grit my teeth and bear them? We must
recognize God's sovereignty, but we also are to actively
address the things that face us.

A good evidence of this balance is seen in the
experience of Paul's thorn in the flesh (2 Corinthians
17:7-10). First, we know it was a messenger of Satan, but
that doesn't mean it wasn't God's will. Satan often is used
by God to accomplish His purposes (e.g., Job's trials,
Christ's crucifixion, etc.). Paul trusted God's sovereignty,
but he also actively sought the Lord's will in the situation.
Three times he asked the Lord to take it away. When he
finally discerned that this thorn was God's will, he had
peace (Philippians 4:6,7) and became content.

So when we encounter divinely designed circumstances, we are to actively seek the Lord about them, and
when the signposts start lining up, we will discern His will.

After receiving the crushing blow of my job rejec-
tion, I first responded by getting angry and bitter toward

the committee. After all, was drawing names out of a hat any way to make important decisions? As I sought the Lord, however, and spent time in the Word, God reminded me that He is sovereign. I could make myself miserable focusing on the secondary causes, or I could trust God's sovereignty and know He can use anything and anyone to lead us. Proverbs 16:33 became a great comfort: "The lot is cast into the lap, but every decision is from the LORD."

Now, I'm not advising you to cast lots in making your decisions. Scripture presents many better and more mature ways to do that, but when life casts lots for you, trust that your sovereign Lord is able to direct the decision for your best. To me, God's sovereignty is one of His most attractive attributes. When it is coupled with His love and grace, it provides tremendous reassurance to the believer.

Why did God detour me from such a promising situation working with my good friend and mentor?

Because He is sovereign. He can see the things I can't see, and He knows what I need more than I do. We don't always get the chance to see clearly why God detours us, but in this case I did. Within a couple of months God clarified His leading me to join the staff of Campus Crusade for Christ.

Not only did God's detour protect me from suffering the consequences of a wrong choice, but it also provided for me in so many ways. What God detoured me to was a ministry that challenged me and stretched me in immeasurable ways. In my first two years on staff at the University of Virginia I was able to help plant a ministry at James Madison University that continues and thrives to this day. Most of the young men I invested my life in while on staff are now either in full-time Christian ministry or having a significant impact as laymen.

Later as director of Campus Crusade's ministry at the University of Tennessee, I was responsible for a ministry team of twelve full-time workers, an opportunity few pastors ever have. I was able, through our campus ministry, to be used in far broader ways than the church position would have provided, and that breadth of experience has been invaluable. Years later, when God moved me back onto the path of church ministry, I realized those experiences had done much to prepare me. God's detour protected me, and it provided for me as only His will can.

□□□

Application Notes

Ask yourself these questions, and write the answers you believe will help you the most. Be honest!

1. What "open doors" or God-given barriers are there to consider in my situation?

2. What trials or difficult circumstances do I need to seek the Lord about?

3. What is God saying to me through these circumstances?

(You may need to come back to these as you work
through other signposts in this book.)

9

Signpost #7

The REST AREA Sign: Peace

□□□□□

I just have a peace about it, Eddie," Bob related. "I feel like this is the right thing to do." I had some questions about his wanting to back out of his commitment to go to the mission field, but this comment effectively shut my mouth. What else could I say? I strongly believe that every Christian is able to hear from God. We don't need an intermediary to tell us what God's will is, and yet I felt concern about Bob's decision.

I had known Bob for several years and we were good friends. No one was more excited than I when he told me he sensed God calling him to serve overseas. We had attended a Christian conference together, and at the end

Bob had surrendered every area of his life to Christ's control, including his plans for the future. It wasn't a great emotional experience. Rather, it was the culmination of all he was learning from the Word and of finally grasping that the most important things in life are the things that will last for eternity.

In the weeks and months that followed, God began to point Bob toward missions. He saw the eternal importance of fulfilling the great commission as he studied the Scriptures. He sensed God tugging at his heart as he prayed. Others advised that his success in his personal ministry on campus showed that God could use him. Everything seemed to be pointing toward full-time Christian work. Even his parents, who he thought would be against the idea, surprised him with their support. He had applied with a missions agency and had been accepted to fill a post in Kenya. After graduation he would go through six months of training, and after he raised his financial support, he would report to language school. Everything seemed to be falling into place.

Now some six months later, as graduation neared, Bob wasn't so sure. He had begun having doubts. His initial excitement had given way to many fears. "How will I ever find a wife in Kenya? I've never raised money before . . . I'm not sure I like the idea of asking people I don't know to give money . . . For that matter, I'm not too excited about asking my friends either."

In the stress and busyness of finals and graduation, Bob hadn't had much time to pray about it. In fact, he hadn't had much time to pray at all. His quiet times had been reduced to a quick couple of verses as he left for class. When he thought about going into ministry, he felt nervous and anxious, not excited. *Maybe that really isn't God's will,* he thought. *Maybe I just talked myself into it before.*

He was already wavering on the fence when the call came from his engineering professor telling Bob he was recommending him for a tremendous government job. The more he thought about it, the more Bob believed, *Maybe this is what God wants me to do.* After all, the salary was exceptional. He would be able to give a lot of money to missions. He could stay in town, too. He'd have his friends to hang out with, and he could begin helping out with the youth group at his church. When the word came that he had gotten the job, Bob was ecstatic. He felt this was the confirmation. "I just really have a peace about it, Eddie," he exclaimed as he related his decision. Had Bob found God's will, or had he strayed from it?

REST AREA

The next signpost to consider on our road to God's will is the REST AREA sign. One of the biblical synonyms of God's peace is what Hebrews 4 refers to as "rest." The REST AREA sign is one of the most important we will talk about, partly because it is one of the most misunderstood and therefore one of the most misapplied. Because the concept of God's peace is linked to favorable emotions in most people's minds, it is often viewed as a feeling instead of a spiritual state of rest. Thus viewed, it becomes a subjective discipline instead of an objective criteria for discerning God's leading.

What God's Peace Is Not

Before we try to nail down what God's peace is, it will be extremely helpful to establish some parameters of what it is not. Having made these eliminations, it will be easier to hone in on exactly what God's peace is.

The first and most essential distinction I've seen is that *God's peace is not circumstantial.* When Jesus spoke of His peace He said, "Not as the world gives, do I give to you" (John 14:27). The peace of the world is dictated always and only by circumstances. Scripture teaches us that God's peace is produced by the Holy Spirit, not by our circumstances (Galatians 5:22,23). This is borne out by the experience of saints throughout the ages. The peace of God, not circumstances, gave Stephen the confidence to preach truth as men took up stones to kill him. The peace of God, not circumstances, enabled Martin Luther to stand firm before the papal authority at the Diet of Worms. No, most certainly, God's peace is not based on favorable circumstances.

I saw this principle some time back when my wife and I were flying home from the Southern Baptist Convention in New Orleans. We had just flown over Montgomery on our way to Atlanta when suddenly the plane banked sharply to the right and began dropping. Nothing was said over the loudspeakers but everyone knew something was seriously wrong. Stewardesses were falling all over the place as they tried frantically to secure everything that was loose. Our ears ached and our stomachs floated from the rapid, corkscrewlike drop in altitude. Babies were screaming and some adults wept openly while still others prayed out loud. My wife's knuckles were white as she gripped my hand.

In less than five minutes we dropped from an altitude of 30,000 feet and approached a small airport. As we prepared to land we saw the fire engines, police cars and National Guard on the ground awaiting us. Once we landed we discovered that a bomb threat had been called in on our flight, and once we all had run safely to a nearby hangar, a cheer went up in unison. As our plane had descended, nothing in our circumstances dictated peace, yet my heart was flooded with it. I felt no anxiety, no fear. Whatever awaited us, my heart was at peace. The world does not give that peace.

The second observation I see is that *God's peace is not always logical.* It doesn't always make sense to us humans. Philippians 4:7 tells us that the peace of God "surpasses all comprehension." This doesn't mean that God's peace is illogical, but that it goes beyond mere human logic. Man's logic fails to factor in the power and sovereignty of God, something even believers don't fully understand or comprehend, and unbelievers can't decipher at all.

Some time ago, my wife and I began having discipline problems with our oldest boy Blake, then four and a half. It seemed that whatever we said, he did the opposite. We would give him instructions and he would look right at us and disobey. It was as if our words didn't even register. These discipline problems had appeared so suddenly and were so uncharacteristic that my wife and I were left scratching our heads. What appeared suddenly in our son's behavior, however, soon spread to his health. Within a matter of a few days he went from an active, energetic four-year-old to total lethargy. He began to lose his motor skills and control of his bladder. He couldn't speak in any way but in a slow whisper. Our family physician immediately referred us to a neurosurgeon and we were prepared for the worst — a possible brain tumor.

As if our son's health weren't enough to trust God with, we suffered added financial burdens as well. On the way to the doctor, the engine of our car blew out. We had been saving for some time to buy a house and a week before had put a $1000 deposit on one. With the car repairs and medical bills, our down-payment savings were gone quickly, and we had to face forfeiting our deposit and not buying a house. In circumstances like these you learn to live just in the present. You take each day as it comes; you face each problem as it comes. The present is enough to trust God for without piling the future on as well.

As we endeavored to live in the present, we found ourselves holding our son's hands and praying as his lethargic and limp body was motored into the brain scan machine. As we prayed for our son, we acknowledged that he belonged to God and we thanked God for giving him to us as long as he did. As we relinquished him to God, our hearts were flooded with a delicious sense of peace. We didn't know what the outcome would be, but we knew it lay in the hands of One we could trust. This was not logical peace from a human perspective, it wasn't man's peace—it was God's, and He doesn't give as the world gives.

One of the reasons God's peace doesn't always make sense at first is because *God sees things that we don't.* He already knew what we would later find out—that our son's problem was not a tumor, but viral encephalitis, a rare problem of a virus taking a wrong turn in the body and ending up in the nervous system. It results in inflammation and swelling of the brain, and God knew that although it sometimes results in permanent brain damage, in this case the recovery would be 100 percent! God also knew that although we didn't have the money to put down on our house, He would soon provide it through a surprise gift of $5,000. God's peace is not illogical—it is beyond mere human logic because it looks from His vantage point, not ours.

What God's Peace Is

Well, we've seen what God's peace is not. It is not based on circumstances, and it is not always logical humanly speaking. Then what is it? The best single description of God's peace is found in John 14:27, a verse I alluded to earlier. In it Jesus says:

> Peace I leave with you; My peace I give to you; not as the world gives, do I give to you. Let not your heart be troubled, nor let it be fearful.

This verse relates an important distinction that demands notice: *God's peace must be differentiated from the peace of the world.* The world can give a certain peace, but it is based on our circumstances and experienced in our feelings. God's peace is based on our being in the center of His will, and it is experienced not in our feelings, but in our spirit.

In a nutshell, *God's peace is the absence of a troubled heart.* Like a diamond displayed on black velvet, it is most clearly seen when contrasted to difficult circumstances.

"But how does this kind of peace guide me toward God's will?" one would logically ask. It is important to recognize that *peace or rest is a spiritual state, a position of everything being right in my relationship with God.* If I am not obeying His leadings and His commands, my spirit will not know peace. If I am, then peace performs a confirming work in my heart. It is, however, subjective and prone to misinterpretation. My experience moves me to conclude that what I believe to be God's guiding peace is most dependable and most to be trusted when it goes against my circumstances. Everywhere peace is presented in Scripture, it is juxtaposed with anxiety. When I am peaceful about something I ought to be anxious about, that is God, not flesh.

Where God's Peace Comes From

Let's look back at Bob's decision. Was he experiencing God's peace or the world's? One of the things that concerned me was that his sense of peace contradicted how God had already led him up to that point. No signpost stands alone, especially not one open to subjective interpretation like this one. As I listened to Bob and looked at his circumstances, I had to ask, "Does the peace you are experiencing come from God or from your circumstances?" That is not a question I as an outsider could answer. Only God and Bob could work it out. In my own decisions, distinguishing between God's peace and the world's has proven very helpful.

How do we get God's peace in our decisions? Scripture gives three specific instructions about how to obtain God's peace that have been an aid to me in my decision making. First, peace is identified in Galatians 5:22,23 as part of the "fruit of the Spirit": "The fruit of the Spirit is love, joy, *peace.*"

Peace is the fruit of yielding to the Holy Spirit's control in my life. If I am to have God's peace guarding my heart in any decision, He must be in control. If He is not, the only peace I can know is the peace of the world which is bound by circumstances.

Another essential to having God's peace is *keeping my eyes on Him.* Isaiah 26:3 states, "Thou wilt keep him in perfect peace, whose mind is stayed on Thee: because he trusteth in Thee" (KJV). If we don't have peace in our decision, it could mean we have our eyes on circumstances instead of on the Lord. When Bob was seeking the Lord about his career, he had a peace about going into the ministry, but when he looked to his circumstances he no longer had peace. From where I sat it appeared that his lack of peace about raising support to go into missions wasn't from God but from his circumstances. God's peace comes from keeping our eyes on Him and trusting in Him.

The third essential to obtaining God's peace is *prayer.* We talked about this in a previous chapter but let's review it here. Philippians 4:6,7 tells us that instead of being anxious, we are to pray, and the result will be that "the peace of God, which surpasses all comprehension, shall guard your hearts and your minds in Christ Jesus." Anxiety may be an indication that something is not God's will, but more often in my life it is a result of not adequately praying about a matter and putting it into God's hands, or a result of taking it back from a position of being surrendered to God. This anxiety is not God's leading but the world's worry. To which one would you attribute Bob's concern about going into missions?

What God's Peace Does

As I related in the chapter on prayer, God's peace is for a purpose. Philippians 4:7 tells us that when we have adequately prayed and surrendered an issue or a decision to God, His peace will guard our hearts and minds. The Greek word translated "guard" is a military term and refers to building a garrison to protect something. That is what

God's peace does in the decision-making process. The power of God's peace protects my heart from fainting, from weakening, and it also protects my mind, literally, my thoughts, guarding them from anxiety.

Not only does God's peace guard me, but it also guides me. In 2 Corinthians 2:12,13 we see that Paul had all the right circumstances to minister in Troas, but God led him otherwise:

> Now when I came to Troas for the gospel of Christ and when a door was opened for me in the Lord, I had no rest for my spirit, not finding Titus my brother; but taking my leave of them, I went on to Macedonia.

Paul had an open door, but he did not have God's peace. He had the right circumstances to minister and the world's peace would have said to stay. But God's peace dictated otherwise. God's peace will guide us if we understand how to distinguish it from the world's circumstantial peace.

Some Dangers With This Signpost

As with every signpost, this one affords opportunities for misapplication. As I alluded to earlier, if we don't have peace about something, it may be that God is not leading us in that direction. However, in my experience with counseling others about God's will, I see a more prevalent reason for lack of peace in the decision-making process: lack of trust in God. Isaiah 26:3 tells us: "Thou wilt keep him in perfect peace, whose mind is stayed on Thee: *because he trusteth in Thee*" (KJV, emphasis mine). Hebrews 4:2 tells us that some do not experience God's positional rest because of unbelief. This verse refers directly to unbelievers, but later the passage (verse 11) applies the principle to believers. To experience God's rest, a synonym for peace, we must trust Him.

Another common danger in understanding God's peace is, it is so easy to misinterpret a lack of stress or problems as that peace. As we saw before, peace that is truly from God is not dictated by circumstances. It is not external. It is internal, and often in stark contrast to outside circumstances.

As we look back at Bob's decision, we must ask ourselves, "Was he being guided by God's peace or by good circumstances?" God can and does use circumstances to direct us, so circumstances being good does not mean something is not God's will. It does not, however, automatically mean that something *is* God's will, either.

In Bob's case, although circumstances pointed toward the good job, many other things had already pointed in another direction. The real enemy of God's best isn't usually something bad but something good—that isn't God's will.

◻◻◻

Applying the Principles

Where are you in your search for God's will? Can you identify with Bob and his confusion over his circumstances? Ask yourself the questions that begin on the next page as you evaluate where you are, and apply this principle of peace as you seek to determine God's will.

1. Do I have a continued inner peace as I pray and consider the other signposts?

2. Do I have a sense of rest, allowing God to do the work, or do I sense the anxiety of me trying to make things work out?

3. What evidence is there that my "peace," or lack of it, is merely circumstantial?

Why not take a moment to make sure your eyes are on the Lord and not your circumstances, and reaffirm your trust in Him? As a future encouragement, write your prayer in the space below:

10

Signpost #8

The NO RIGHT TURN Sign: The Holy Spirit

❑❑❑❑❑

W hat should I pray, Lord?" I silently implored. I had been trying for some time to pray for my brother, but I just didn't know what to pray. He had been arrested at the Atlanta airport with a suitcase full of cocaine and money.

My brother and I had grown up close. Being the only children of a broken marriage, we looked out for each other. Early in life, I started into drugs when I found out he did them, but when I became a Christian as a freshman in college all of that changed for me. It didn't change for him, though.

The lawyer had told us that since this was his second offense, we should be prepared for a fifteen- to thirty-year sentence. My heart was heavy and burdened, but the harder I tried to pray the harder the words came. I didn't want my brother to go to prison, but as I prayed that he wouldn't, I knew in my heart it wasn't right. His first drug conviction resulted in three years probation, and this second conviction proved he had learned nothing from the first time. If he got off free this time, would he keep going the same direction? That really wasn't even a question to be asked, though, because we all knew he wasn't going to get off free. But how should I pray?

There is no simple way to explain what happened next, but as clearly as if it were out loud, I heard a voice in my spirit. The thought was planted in my mind: *Pray for a sentence of only five years.*

Now, before you start thinking twilight zone or loony bin, let me assure you this is not a regular occurrence in my spiritual life. Usually when God speaks to me, He does so through His saints or through the Scriptures. On this occasion, however, God, by the Holy Spirit, spoke to me in my spirit. If you have never experienced that, I'm not sure I can help you understand what I mean, but God spoke and I knew it was from Him.

During the next few weeks I asked every believer I knew to join me in praying that my brother would get only a five-year sentence. I shared this request with my church. I shared it with my Bible study group. I shared it with my roommates. I shared it with the Christian group I was involved in on campus. I asked every Christian I came in contact with to join me in trusting God for this very specific request. As the trial neared, my confidence grew, because I knew the petition I was placing before God did not originate with me.

Finally the verdict came. On each of three counts my brother was to receive a ten-year sentence, but they were to run concurrently, the first five years in jail, the second five on probation. God took the most roundabout way possible to give my brother a five-year prison sentence. In the process, He greatly encouraged my faith and that of those around me, especially my family. Those days of my brother's incarceration were hard on my family, and of course especially on my brother, but God used them to do a real work of reconciliation both in my brother's relationship with God and in his relationship with the family. God does sometimes speak His will by that "still, small voice" of the Spirit.

NO RIGHT TURN

The next signpost on the way to God's will is the NO RIGHT TURN sign. In Isaiah 30:21 we are given a glimpse of one of the ways God speaks His will:

> And your ears will hear a word behind you, "This is the way, walk in it" whenever you turn to the right or to the left.

I have experienced that voice, not often, but at crucial junctures in my spiritual walk. As we consider ways God speaks His will, do not underestimate the possibility that He may speak it by His Spirit who indwells us. I link that with the NO RIGHT TURN sign because most often we hear the voice of the Spirit, not when we are on the path of God's will, but when we turn from it "to the right or to the left" as Isaiah points out.

The Leading of the Holy Spirit

To understand better the leading of the Holy Spirit, it will be helpful if we understand more about the Holy Spirit Himself and consider how He ministers.

As a child, I found the concept of the Holy Spirit difficult to understand. When we sang "Praise Father, Son and Holy Ghost" at church, my juvenile mind conjured up an image of Casper the Friendly Ghost with a halo. The Scriptures make it clear, however, that the Holy Spirit is a person, not an amorphous, impersonal force. He is as much God as Jesus or the Father, yet He is often the most misunderstood person of the Trinity.

The Word of God clarifies several ways the Holy Spirit works in our lives. Perhaps the most relevant passage to the subject of God's will is Romans 8:14: "All who are being *led by the spirit of God* . . . are sons of God." If I am a child of God, I will experience the Holy Spirit's leading. That is not open to discussion. This doesn't mean I always follow, but if I do not experience the Spirit's leading, I am not a Christian. Jesus told the unbelieving Jews, "You do not believe, because you are not of My sheep. My sheep hear My voice, and I know them, and they follow Me" (John 10:26,27).

But how exactly do we hear His voice? One of the ways is, as I related above, by His Spirit who lives within us. That is what I experienced when I sought God's will in how to pray for my brother.

John 16:7-9 tells us that the Holy Spirit *leads by conviction in three specific areas: sin, righteousness, and judgment.* The same Spirit who first convinced me of the truth of the gospel indwells me and lets me know when I stray from God's desire. He points me in the direction of righteousness. And when I stubbornly go my own way, He reminds me of judgment. Conviction is one way God speaks His will.

Another ministry of the Holy Spirit is, He *teaches us and reminds us of God's truth.*

On Christ's last evening with the disciples, He spent most of His time helping them understand the ministry of the coming Holy Spirit. The result is the richest and fullest teaching in all of Scripture on the person of the Holy Spirit (John 14 – 16). One of the points Christ makes in this powerful passage is that He, our "Helper" as Christ called Him, "will teach you all things, and bring to remembrance all that I said to you" (John 14:26). It is through the work of the Holy Spirit that we understand the truths of God's Word. It is also through His ministry that pertinent Scriptures are called to mind when we need them. We see this ministry illustrated numerous times in the lives of the apostles.

This ministry of the Holy Spirit calling to mind Scripture at my time of need is what Paul refers to in Ephesians 6:17 when he speaks of the "sword of the Spirit, which is the word of God." In Greek, what is translated "word" here is not *logos,* the general term normally used. Instead Paul uses *rhema,* indicating "spoken words," Scriptures which God speaks to our heart by His Spirit as we need them. Often as we seek God's will about a choice we are to make or a path we want to pursue, He answers us by the Holy Spirit calling to our mind a verse that tells us what we need to know.

In Christ's upper-room discourse, He also revealed another way the Holy Spirit ministers: by revealing and disclosing truth. John 16:13-15 teaches us that the Holy Spirit is able to "guide you into all the truth . . . He shall take of Mine, and shall disclose it to you."

Of course, this revealing and disclosing ministry relates to the Bible and never contradicts the clear teaching of the Scriptures. Sometimes, however, as with my need for wisdom in how to pray for my brother, the Holy Spirit discloses God's wisdom to our hearts in a specific way to guide us.

Some Dangers With This Signpost

As with each of the signposts directing us to God's will, this one is not without its dangers. Hearing the voice of the Spirit and recognizing His leading is contingent on several factors. First, although all believers can hear and recognize the voice of their Shepherd, in my own life *that process becomes easier as I mature in my walk with Christ.* Hearing and recognizing His voice implies a relationship. For my relationship with Christ to be effective, it must be developed.

Second, to hear and recognize the voice of God requires *keeping short accounts with Him about sin.* If there is sin in my life and I know it but have not dealt with it God's way, the only word I will hear from God is conviction of that sin. Any other voice I hear will not be God's, but the voice of the world, my flesh, or the devil.

This unholy trio speaks louder when my walk with Christ is dirtied by sin, and any one of them can be quite deceiving. Scripture teaches that Satan sometimes disguises himself as an angel of light, and I must remember that. The surest safeguard to rightly applying this signpost of the Spirit is to make sure my walk with God is healthy and unhindered by sin, and to ask God to confirm His leading with other signposts as well.

A good passage to keep in mind when seeking to follow the Lord is Psalm 32:8,9. It reveals God's commitment to show us His will — and two dangers of missing His leading:

> I will instruct you and teach you in the way which you should go; I will counsel you with My eye upon you.
> Do not be as the horse or as the mule which have no understanding.

A horse tends to run ahead, and the bit and bridle must be pulled to hold him in check. On the other hand, the mule tends to lag behind in stubbornness, and must be dragged and kicked.

Many Christians follow God the same way a horse or a mule does. Either they run ahead of God without waiting to hear from Him, or they lag behind in stubbornness and won't step out in faith. Which is your tendency? Mine is running ahead of God, but I have learned the hard way that it is better to find His will the first time than to be taught it by consequences.

□□□

Applying the Principles

As you seek God's will, remember it is not like an Easter-egg hunt where He has done His best to hide it and you must try to find it. God wants you to know His will even more than you do, and He will show it to you if you let Him. But to hear that "still, small voice," you must monitor your relationship with Him. Consider the following questions and record your answers here:

    1. Do you sense God is motivating you toward or away from a particular course of action? If so, what?

    2. Are you behaving as a horse in this situation (running ahead of God)? If so, what do you need to do differently to take time to listen to Him?

    3. Are you behaving as a mule in this situation (lagging behind because of your stubbornness or unbelief)? If so, what do you need to do differently to take the steps of faith He wants you to?

    4. Are you sure you are filled with the Holy Spirit (Ephesians 5:18) and there is no unconfessed sin in your heart?

    Why not write out a prayer of yieldedness here to confirm your commitment?

11

Signpost #9

The CARPOOL *Sign:*
Stewardship

□□□□□

T o be honest, Steve's comment caught me a little off
guard. Someone had asked him how God led him
to join the staff of Campus Crusade for Christ. I
was still very young in the Lord and somewhat naïve in
this matter of how God communicated His will, and I must
admit that at first I was a little disappointed with his
response.

"There were many things to consider," he said, "but
the major issue for me came down to stewardship."

I had expected something far more dramatic, like a
dream or a vision at the end of an all-night prayer vigil. It
seemed to me that God calling someone to the ministry

ought to be a special, almost mystical experience. Stewardship certainly didn't fit my perception.

The group inquired further and Steve explained the process he had gone through to determine God's will for his vocation. In college, he majored in business and he planned to get his MBA after graduation. Through his involvement in Campus Crusade during his undergraduate years, he had introduced several classmates to Christ and had a discipleship group that God had blessed tremendously. In fact, all three of the young men he discipled in his last two years of college now had disciples of their own.

During the summers, Steve had participated in missions projects, one in a resort area in California, and two overseas. He felt the training and experience of those projects made a profound impact on his walk with Christ and his personal ministry. He also attended numerous Campus Crusade conferences and further developed his evangelism and discipleship skills.

Toward the end of his junior year, Steve began thinking about full-time ministry. During the orientation for his missions project that summer, one of the leaders made a statement that startled him. The leader said, "I realize that many of you may feel inadequate to minister in some of the situations you will find yourselves. The truth is, though, that you already know more about the Bible and have more ministry experience than most of the pastors you will be working with in this part of Africa."

Steve had never considered himself a spiritual giant by any stretch of the imagination, yet he was surprised to learn that only about 5 percent of Christians have a personal ministry, less than 2 percent share their faith on a regular basis, and only 1 percent disciple others to do these things.

On his missions project, Steve worked with an African national named Idirishu. Everything in Idirishu's life was surrendered to the Lord and to the cause of reaching his countrymen for Christ, and he was a challenge to be around.

Steve asked him what motivated him to minister, and Idirishu answered, "I am wanting to be found a faithful steward. Everything I have, God has given to me, and one day I will answer to Him for how I used it. When I have money, I must spend it in ways that honor Him. The time I have must be managed like money. The truth God teaches me, I am a steward of, and I must share it with others."

"That last statement spoke to me the most," Steve told us. "I never really considered that what God had taught me was as much something to be a steward of as my time or money or abilities."

As Steve related, 2 Timothy 2:2 tells us that we are to entrust the truth God teaches us to "faithful men, who will be able to teach others also."

As he applied that principle to his own life, Steve realized that many people around him could be businessmen, but few knew how to have a ministry. "I looked at the biblical teaching and ministry training God had entrusted to me, and it didn't make sense to use it only in my spare time. The needs of the world are too great. Coming on staff seemed the best way to be a good steward of all God had built into my life."

That's when I began to realize that God reveals His will in many different ways.

CARPOOL

The next signpost we encounter on our road to God's will is the CARPOOL sign. It pops up more and more frequently around major cities where pollution is a problem and as gas prices continue to rise. It reminds us to be good stewards of everything we have any control over, including our money and our planet. Godly stewardship, an important principle in the Scriptures, is one area through which God speaks His wisdom.

The Call to Stewardship

The book of Matthew contains what is known as the Olivet Discourse, a conversation Christ had with His disciples. He relates a series of parables, of which one of the most familiar is the Parable of the Talents. You could probably tell it from memory. Three men are given talents (bars of gold or silver) to manage for their master. One receives five talents, one receives two, and one receives only one. As you know, the first two faithfully invested their talents, and when their master returned they had doubled the amounts. The third steward hid his talent and had nothing more when the master returned.

This parable contains an important message for us: We are stewards of all that is entrusted to us, and one day we will give an account. But there is another, less obvious message in this parable. It is found in what was done with the talent managed by the unfaithful steward — it was taken away and given to the faithful steward.

Do you ever wonder why some people seem to get many natural opportunities to share Christ while others have so few? From what I have observed in ministry, I believe that opportunities to minister are given by God in response to our proven faithfulness. Those who are faithful in the small opportunities to serve receive greater opportunities. Those who aren't lose what opportunities they did have, and they lead insignificant lives. I'm not saying that all worthwhile service is flashy and noticed by others, or that all serve the same way, or that all see the same results. But I am saying that those who are good stewards of the chances to minister which God gives them will lead eternally significant lives even if unnoticed here on earth.

Stewardship and the Will of God

The Bible assures us that part of God's will for our lives is to be good stewards of all He entrusts to us. The question to ask ourselves is, Will this decision I am making result in my being a good steward? Perhaps I am considering a purchase. Would that purchase demonstrate good stewardship of the money God entrusts to me? Perhaps I am trying to decide on something involving a substantial time commitment. Will this decision reflect good stewardship of my time? As we can see from Steve's experience, understanding stewardship becomes an important resource in evaluating career choices.

What a Steward Is a Steward of

If I am called to be a steward, and if one day I will give an account to God for my stewardship, then I need to know what I am to be a steward of. The Scriptures spell out four precious commodities which must be managed prudently. Understanding these aids me greatly in knowing God's will for my life.

The first commodity each believer is to be a steward of is *time*. The President of the United States has the same number of hours in his week as I do. A significant life is not a result of how much time I have, but of how I use that time. Ephesians 5:15,16 exhorts us, "Therefore be careful how you walk, not as unwise men, but as wise, making the most of your time, because the days are evil."

Time is a perishable commodity; it is not eternal. Once used, it is gone forever, leaving in its place what I traded it for. A good evaluation question is, Was it worth it? Was my use of that time worth what I have to show for it? The key here is balance. For example, I can't use stewardship as an excuse for not sleeping or not spending time with my family. I must balance my priorities.

The next area of stewardship is my *talents*. Every person has certain God-given abilities, both natural and spiritual, that make him unique, and God desires that those abilities be used to the fullest. A year or so ago a young man asked my advice on what he should do when he graduated from college. He had some job prospects, but he was also a world-class distance runner and could make a living for a while doing that. As I helped him through the process of making the decision, I reminded him of this issue of stewardship. While stewardship alone didn't guarantee it was God's will for him to continue running, it certainly was a major factor. Few of us can lay claim to being a world-class anything, much less a world-class athlete. I encouraged him to consider the tremendous platform for ministry which athletics brings and to ask God if that might be His will for now. His business degree could be picked up later, but his running couldn't.

Certainly natural abilities such as athletic prowess or artistic giftedness are resources to be managed, but not all of us have significant talents in those areas. Scripture teaches, however, that every believer does have spiritually endowed abilities that God calls Him to be a steward of. The Bible refers to these as "spiritual gifts." In 1 Peter 4:10 we are told: "As each one has received a special gift, employ it in serving one another, as good stewards of the manifold grace of God."

Our spiritual gifts can be neglected (1 Timothy 4:14), or they can be developed (2 Timothy 1:6). To be good stewards we must exercise those gifts in such a way that they minister to others, not just ourselves (1 Peter 4:10), and they must glorify God, not us (1 Peter 4:11).

For Steve, both his abilities and his gift were important factors in his career choice, as they are for all of us. Almost every profession has certain required abilities or gifts that not everyone else has. Not all of us, even with the same effort, could play pro football. How are you gifted? What are your strengths and abilities? God will call you to account for how you use them.

The third area of stewardship, perhaps the most often mentioned aspect, is stewardship of our *treasures,* the financial resources we are given, or that we develop. Like time, money is also a perishable commodity, once used it is gone, leaving behind what it was traded for. It is not eternal, but, like time, it can be invested in things that are eternal.

Also, like time, it can be wasted. Luke 16:11,12 relates a somber warning:

> If therefore you have not been faithful in the use of unrighteous mammon, who will entrust the true riches to you? And if you have not been faithful in the use of that which is another's, who will give you that which is your own?

Stewardship of our finances says a lot regarding our decisions.

The fourth dimension of stewardship is an area that often is omitted in sermons on the subject. Most of us have given little thought to this, but God calls every believer also to be a good steward of *truth.*

God, through His servants, has invested truth in every believer. Perhaps some of us know more than others, but all of us have received some truth, and 2 Timothy 2:2 speaks loudly to this issue as Paul exhorts Timothy: "The things which you have heard from me . . . these entrust to faithful men, who will be able to teach others also."

Each of us has seen truth modeled and heard it taught. This truth thus becomes in our lives a treasure to be managed, a stewardship to be entrusted to others who will then do the same with still others — and the Christian faith grows and spreads. This directive is echoed in the Great Commission recorded in Matthew 28:18-20. Christ commands us to be "teaching them to observe all that I commanded you."

We are stewards of all that God has built into our lives, and we will one day give an account to Him. Knowing this helps me in my decision making. At times it may mean saying no to temporal opportunities in favor of eternal ones. Being a faithful steward of God's truth may mean I don't climb the corporate ladder as fast or as high as others whose only commitment is to the company or to themselves. God's will for me may not mean I'm the top salesman or the youngest junior partner, but whatever it does mean will be good, and acceptable, and perfect (Romans 12:2).

What Is Required of a Steward?

Each of us is a steward; that is already settled. The question of the Christian life, then, is, What kind of steward am I? Since Scripture makes it certain that one day I will give an account to God for my life, the admonition of 1 Corinthians 4:2 ought to ring loudly in my ears: "Moreover, it is required of stewards that one be found trustworthy." If I am a trustworthy steward, if I have been found faithful, I will be rewarded. If I am unfaithful, my salvation is still secure, but reward is forfeited and I will "suffer loss" (1 Corinthians 3:10-15).

Some Dangers of Misapplication

Stewardship is one way God guides me in the decisions of life, but it comes with a warning. In order for stewardship to be effective in my decisions, I must be operating on an eternal value system. I must place the highest premium on the things that are important to God and that will last in eternity. Otherwise my scales of decision will be unbalanced. If I weigh temporal values such as pleasure, success, achievement, etc., too heavily, then I will draw wrong conclusions about God's leading. Stewardship speaks with the voice and values of God, and if His values are not mine, my going will not be with His guiding.

□□□

Applying the Principles

As we saw in Steve's decision to go into ministry instead of business, stewardship can be one of the ways God speaks His will. Evaluate your decision in light of how it reflects your stewardship of these four key areas of your life, and apply this signpost to your decision-making process:

Stewardship of your *time*

Stewardship of your *talents*

Stewardship of your *treasures*

Stewardship of your *truth*

12

Signpost #10

The NO PARKING Sign: Faith

□□□□□

L ord, am I missing Your will?" I quietly prayed. "I know that if I turn from Your will, I am turning to a lie, so what should I do, Lord?" As I stammered out these silent supplications, my heart reeled in turmoil. It was the culmination of weeks of agonizing about a decision I had made two months earlier. I had decided to leave my position directing Campus Crusade's ministry at the University of Tennessee and accept a job as an associate pastor of a church. I handed in my resignation over Christmas to give time for a replacement to be found, and I was finishing out the school year. With so much time to think about it, I began to wonder if I had made the right decision.

I had been working with Campus Crusade for Christ for more than six years and now felt that God wanted to move me on. I had committed to the Lord, however, that I would not leave my present ministry without a clear sense of calling from Him to something else. Life has effectively taught me that the only place to find joy and peace is in the middle of God's will. Nowhere else satisfies.

It seemed that the direction I was heading and the decision I had made were following the leadings of God. But I had second thoughts—major second thoughts. I feared the consequences of leaving God's will, but I was so far along in the process, I couldn't back out now. My house was up for sale. My job had been assigned to someone else for the next year. I had told all my friends confidently I was following God in leaving the staff and moving to a church. I was also anxious about stepping from a significant ministry into an unknown area of church work. Was I really following God? Or was I just tired of walking by faith? Had I been lured away from God's leading by the promise of a steady salary I didn't have to raise? How did I get to this point?

As I hung my head in a humble spirit of prayer, I thought back over the events of the past year that had brought me to this place. I had always desired to work in a local church and long suspected that my gifts of teaching and leading were better suited for that service, and the past summer that desire deepened and became more defined. As a culmination to books I read, prayers I prayed and Scriptures I studied, God began to give me a specific vision for my life. I was convinced that the world would not be reached for Christ with so little of our Christian manpower tapped. I was frustrated and burdened by the great number of Christians in local churches across America whose faith is largely a spectator sport. In the average local church only about 5 percent of the people have a personal ministry.

As God began to knit these perspectives and passions together, I began asking Him to open the door for me to move to the local church. I began praying for an opportunity to be a part of a new reformation of local churches moving people toward ministry. I began trusting God to put me in a situation where I not only could have a local ministry but also could serve as a catalyst to other churches.

About this time a pastor friend named Wayne Barber contacted me regarding a position at his church. Whenever I had thought about local church ministry, I often thought of brother Wayne. I had met him five years earlier and liked him immediately. He was a strong and gifted expository teacher of the Scriptures. In fact, he was the principle male teacher alongside Kay Arthur for Precept Upon Precept Ministries, an international Bible-teaching outreach.

Wayne's church was as close as any I had ever seen to what I believe the biblical model to be. He and I thought so much alike, and we dreamed so much alike. In fact, just after I first met him I asked the Lord to let me serve with him some day.

Wayne's call was the right person, the right place, and the right time. The only problem was, it wasn't the right position. He asked me to consider coming as youth pastor for junior high through college age rather than in the area of evangelism and discipleship, a position I was believing God for but which they already had filled. It wasn't what I was expecting.

I knew I could relate with the college students, but I wasn't so sure about the high schoolers, and I was scared to death at the thought of junior highers. Would I be able to relate with them? Would I really be able to minister? To be honest, I was disappointed. But I so wanted to work with Wayne, and I did feel God was leading me to the local church. Maybe this was His way of moving me toward where He ultimately wanted me to be.

After much prayer, I concluded that this was in fact what He wanted me to do, and He would make me adequate for the task. And then, sooner or later, He would turn my ministry in the direction of discipleship and evangelism. All I needed at that time was to step out in faith and trust Him to work things out His way. So I did. I accepted the position, and I handed my resignation in to Campus Crusade.

But, as I said, now I wasn't so sure. This nagging sense of doubt dulled my zeal and clouded my thoughts — in my mind the title "Youth Pastor" sounded so insignificant, like stepping aside from the real cause of Christ to babysit. "What should I do, Lord?"

Minute after agonizing minute went by as I finally came to the point of complete surrender. "Lord, whatever You want me to do, I'll do it. If You want me to turn this church job down, I'll do it today. If You want me to ask for my old job back, I'll do it. If I can't get it back, I'll trust You with it. Whatever You want, Lord, just show me."

I sat silently, half expecting God to confirm that I had missed His will. Instead, He began bringing to my mind the many ways He had already confirmed His leading. Soon I realized I already knew God's will even if I didn't fully understand it. I just needed to keep walking by faith.

NO PARKING

The next sign we encounter on the way to God's will is the NO PARKING sign. One of the overriding principles of the Christian life is that it is a walk of faith. This is especially significant in determining God's will. Many times God asks us to take a step of faith before He shows us what He is up to. Often further revelation of His will follows when we have taken the steps of faith commensurate with His present leading.

One of our biggest dangers is parking by sight instead of moving by faith. In the Christian life, sometimes God slows us down by telling us to wait, but we should never park.

God's Will Is a Process

Sometimes the way to where God is leading us is not "as the crow flies." Discerning God's will is not merely figuring out where He wants us, but following as He leads us. His leading may involve detours; it may involve rest stops. He may even take us aside to teach us and to prepare us for where He will lead later.

You see, God's will is not a *point,* but a *process.*

The process of a Christian walk can be broken down and dissected into specific points. It is a process of learning, a process of growing, a process not simply of doing, but of becoming. Many times we make the mistake of seeking God's will only in the major decisions, the crisis points. But effectiveness at these times is linked to the ongoing process of following Christ in everyday things.

Solomon describes this principle of God's will as being a process instead of just a point in Proverbs 3:5,6: "Trust in the LORD with all your heart, and do not lean on your own understanding. In all your ways acknowledge Him, and He will make your paths straight."

Do you notice the repetition of the word *all?* Major decisions are much more difficult when we haven't involved God in the minor ones. "Trust in the Lord with *all* your heart" indicates a relationship, not simply instructions to follow. "In *all* your ways acknowledge Him" reflects the fact that following God in the minor decisions makes us more receptive to Him in the major ones. When we do that, we have the promise that "He will make our paths straight [clear or right]." Major decisions will not become major headaches.

I like the way Paul Little expresses this principle of process in his booklet *Affirming the Will of God* (Inter-Varsity, n.d.). Let's look at it again:

> The will of God is not like a magic package let down from heaven by a string . . . the will of God is far more like a scroll that unrolls every day . . . the will of God is something to be discerned and lived out every day of our lives. It is not something to be grasped as a package once for all. Our call, therefore, is basically not to follow a plan or a blueprint, or to go to a place or take up a work, but rather to follow the Lord Jesus Christ.

If we seek God's will only at the crisis points, why even bother? Of what value can His leading be in the major decisions if we have not followed His wisdom in the minor ones?

Why God's Will Is a Process

Why do you think God makes His will a process? Why doesn't He just hand out road maps and send us on our way?

The answer is complex but not complicated.

First of all, think about your own life. What would it be like if you knew right now where God wanted you to be in twenty years? How would such knowledge affect the here and now? If you are like me, knowing the future would make it much harder to live in the present. I would be tempted to take shortcuts. For example, if I knew at age 20 who God wanted me to marry, why bother dating anyone else? Yet dating other people helped me to become who I needed to be in my marriage. If I knew before I took a job that it was a dead end, would I still take it? How would I have *learned the lessons I needed* without that process? If I knew before I ran a race that I would lose, would I still run? If we knew the end from the beginning, it would be all too easy to let our "logic" supersede God's leading.

Another reason God's will is a process is that *tomorrow's assignments cannot be handled with today's faith.* If I knew that tomorrow held martyrdom for me, would I be able to take the steps today that lead to that path? Today's process builds my faith for tomorrow's assignments. It is faithfulness in the little things today that makes me sturdy enough to be faithful in the big things tomorrow. In the Sermon on the Mount Jesus said, "Do not be anxious for tomorrow; for tomorrow will care for itself. Each day has enough trouble of its own" (Matthew 6:34).

I think this attitude must have been what He was getting at. Remember: How do you walk a mile? One step at a time. There is no other way.

Understanding this reality of God's will being a process enabled me to say yes to a detour and to accept a job that didn't seem in line with my long-term direction. But my commitment to the process of God's will also caused me to have second thoughts. None of us is always on track. None of us makes all the right decisions. None of us never strays into sin. That is why God's will must be a process—*it allows imperfect people to keep coming back.*

You Have to Keep Moving

As I sought God in the middle of my process, He confirmed that I was on the right track. I just needed to keep trusting and keep moving. This underscores one of the big dangers we spoke of earlier—parking. Have you ever done it? I have, many times.

We sit back and look for everything to work out before we go any further. The problem is, if you are sitting in a parked car, it is hard to know which way your tires are turned. But once you start moving, you know which way they are headed and you can make corrections if necessary. Following God is like that. Sometimes it takes a step of faith to see which way we are heading, but once we do, we see more clearly where we are to go.

It is also easier to turn the steering wheel once the car is moving. Following God is a lot like that. It is much easier for Him to redirect us if we are moving than to turn us if we are standing still. That is another indication that following God's will is a process. I had to shift out of park and get moving. When I did, and I became willing to veer from my course toward the church job, God confirmed that I was then on the right course.

What about you? Is your car in park or in gear? If the process of God's will seems to be at an impasse in your life, maybe it's because you aren't moving.

A Hindrance to Doing God's Will

The principle hindrance in the process of following God is that we tend to pull away from leadings that require steps of faith. It is easier to say yes to something that appeals to my flesh than something that appeals to my spirit, because following God means taking steps of faith, and my flesh doesn't like that. Paul puts it this way: "We walk by faith, not by sight" (2 Corinthians 5:7). Walking by sight means I can figure out all the angles; everything makes sense; everything fits. Walking by faith means trusting God even if I can't figure out all the angles, even if nothing makes sense — but my flesh doesn't like to do that. What about you?

If, like me, you sometimes struggle with taking steps of faith, perhaps the conclusion of my story will be an encouragement to you. Even though it didn't all make sense, I headed toward the church job by faith. I just had to trust that in time the vision and burden God had given me would come to pass.

I finished my ministry at the University of Tennessee about the second week of May and then packed my family up for a vacation before starting my new job. Several days into our vacation I got a phone call from my boss-to-be, Wayne Barber. The fellow they had hired as Associate Pastor of Discipleship became increasingly frustrated with his job description. He didn't have the vision or desire for discipleship. What he really enjoyed was working with young people. He had served for a number of years as youth pastor at another church. Not knowing where my heart was, Wayne called to see if I would consider trading job descriptions with the other man. When I climbed down from the ceiling, I gave him an enthusiastic yes. God knew all along how things would work out. I just had to trust Him while He clued everyone else in.

The process God took me through taught me much about discerning His will. One of the results is this book, but it is not only the fruit of that process — it is part of the process. One of my desires has been to be a catalyst and to engage in ministry outside my church. Getting this book published is a part of that. I haven't found God's will for my life yet — I'm still following it.

ロロロ

Applying the Principles

What about you? Does this idea of following God's will, instead of just finding it, meet you where you are? Considering each of the following questions and recording your answers will help you apply the signpost of faith to your pursuit of God and His will.

1. What steps of faith does God want me to take in my present decision and circumstances?

2. What steps of faith am I trying to avoid?

3. What specific areas or circumstances in this decision do I have to trust God to work out?

A Prayer

Dear Lord, I want to walk by faith in this decision and not by sight or self-effort. Help me to trust You and lean on You. Make me sensitive to any areas I am not trusting You with and help me to obey. Amen.

13

Signpost #11

The STOP Sign: Waiting

□□□□□

"Do you think we will ever be able to buy a house?" my wife asked in painful honesty.

We had moved to town a few months earlier and were no closer to finding a house we could afford and could fit into than when we first moved. When I accepted the church job, Michele made many trips down to our hometown-to-be. She had grown up there and already knew which areas were safe and liveable and which were not. After several months of looking, she still hadn't found anything acceptable in our price range. We weren't worried, though, and decided to rent a house until we sold our old home.

A couple from our new church had a house for sale and they offered to rent it to us on a month-by-month basis if we were willing to let them leave it on the market. It was located conveniently close to my work, and they gave us a break on the price, so it seemed like a good deal. But the months ticked by and we still couldn't find a permanent home. We became increasingly nervous knowing that at any time someone might buy the house we were renting, and then where would we be?

I think this time of looking and waiting was hardest on my wife. A home she is happy with is so important to a woman. The months of living out of boxes and the continual frustration of looking and finding nothing took their toll. We knew God had called us to be there, and we continued to seek His wisdom and to ask Him to provide, but nothing happened.

Finally, we had a breakthrough. A contractor friend offered to build us a home at a substantial discount. If we could find an acceptable lot in our price range, our new home would immediately be worth more than we paid for it. It took a while, but eventually we stumbled across a half-dozen lots a bank had foreclosed on. They were in our price range and only a few miles from my work. It seemed God had provided at last!

The next few weeks were a whirlwind of activity as we settled on a set of plans, looked at finances, and arranged for the contractor to do the final survey of the lot to make sure everything was okay.

Then the snags began. First, a limitation in the building code of the subdivision required a concrete driveway instead of asphalt. Chi-ching! The cash register rang out—the cost had gone up.

Then we had to agree to a 70-percent brick exterior. Chi-ching! The cost went up some more.

And then there was the extra grading work and the septic tank. Chi-ching!

The straw that broke our financial camel's back came from the water company. The first one hundred feet of water line were free, but there was a small problem. Ours was the last lot on the street, and in order for us to get water service, we would have to pay for water line across four empty lots, to the tune of $3500. Part of this would come back when (and if) the other lots were built on, but we didn't have that kind of money to flex with.

We had to admit that the dream house in our price range wasn't in our price range anymore. My wife's grandparents offered to loan us the difference and give us a couple of years to start paying on it, but the more we prayed about it, the more we became convinced that we were the ones making things happen, not God. We could find no rest in our spirits. We were striving and finagling rather than seeing God answer our prayers.

Finally, after several late-night conversations in bed, my wife and I agreed that building on the lot we'd found was not God's way of meeting our needs. But what was? Sooner or later we would have to find a permanent home. What was the Lord trying to tell us?

STOP

The next signpost we come to as we travel down this road to God's will is the STOP sign. Sometimes as we are seeking God's will, instead of giving us the answer we desire, God says, "Wait." Have you ever experienced that? This is where Michele and I found ourselves at that time. It seemed every direction we turned offered another brick wall. Perhaps no signpost is more difficult to accept gracefully than this one, but the only time we experienced God's peace was when we waited.

In America convenience is king. When we want instant breakfast we just add milk. Dinner goes from the freezer to the microwave to the table in less than ten minutes. When we need instant cash, we have automated teller machines available twenty-four hours a day. If we want a letter to go overnight, we Federal Express it, and if that isn't fast enough, we fax it. From coast-to-coast jet travel to quick-dry nail polish, there is little in our culture that cultivates patience. Small wonder that young people today struggle with waiting until marriage to become sexually active. Yet God quite often calls us to wait. As I read through the Psalms, I am amazed at how many times that annoying word *wait* appears. I think God is trying to tell us something.

Why Wait?

Psalm 37:7 says, "Rest in the LORD and wait patiently for Him." But why? I believe there are many reasons God sends us through "wait training." We need to learn lessons there that cannot be learned anywhere else. When we seek God and His answer seems to be "wait," we don't always hear it because that answer is not the one we are looking for. Michele and I wanted to move into a home, so we weren't always content when God's answer was wait, but He used the process to keep us seeking Him.

One of the lessons God teaches us in "wait training" is to *keep our eyes on Him, not on our circumstances.* One of the real blessings for my wife and me during our nine months of renting was learning that we could experience God's peace and rest even if our circumstances weren't as we liked. When we wait on God for something, that area serves as a continual reminder to keep our eyes on Jesus, something we are always called to do.

Another lesson we learn in waiting is that *the giver is more important than the gift.* A child who always gets what he wants when he wants it is not a grateful child and ultimately isn't happy. Waiting helps us put life in perspective, and often it causes us to come to grips with what we have rather than bemoaning what we don't have. As we look to the Lord for answers, for provision, we realize who He is, and we see that ultimately, "Every good thing bestowed and every perfect gift is from above" (James 1:17). When we wait for something, we appreciate it when it is given, and we also learn to appreciate the one who gives it.

A third thing waiting teaches us is, *there is a difference between needs and wants.* When God calls us to wait, He also calls us to do without for a time. In these times of deprivation we learn what our limits are and what we are capable of handling as human beings. I have known great times of financial blessing and I have known great times of scarcity and, to be honest, I didn't learn much from the blessings. I grew more as a person and as a Christian during adversity than I ever grew in any time of abundance. When we say we "need" a second car, what we really mean is we "want" one. When we say we "need" a bigger house, what we really mean is we "want" one. I'm not saying God never gives us our wants—He has blessed me in immeasurable ways—but part of maturity is learning the difference between what I need and what I want. Waiting teaches me that.

Finally, *waiting demonstrates faith in God instead of in ourselves.* You see, waiting is a choice. It is a decision that says, "I want what God provides." It is a result of volition. It is believing that what God provides is better than what I can do by myself, and surrendering to that. When Michele and I first began looking for a home, we already knew it would be a long-term decision. Barring the Lord's intervention, I expect to be where I am for some time to come. It will take years for my dreams and vision to be realized. Knowing this, we didn't want to settle for a home we would later regret. So we committed to the Lord to wait for what He provided — and I believe He took so long to make sure we really meant it. Waiting is an act of faith.

What about you? Are you waiting on the Lord in your decision? If you aren't, you will find yourself making things happen on your own, and you will ultimately settle for second best. An old saying, popular where I come from, goes like this: "You can have hamburgers at five o'clock or steak at seven." Things worth waiting for usually require waiting. In job choices, in mate choices, in life choices, I have seen people settle for less than the best because they weren't willing to wait. If I am unwilling to wait for God's will, that is what I will forfeit, His will. If I want the good, acceptable, perfect will of God, I will probably be called to wait for it.

Some Key Principles

One key principle we must understand about waiting is that, as God tells the prophet Isaiah,

My thoughts are not your thoughts,
Neither are your ways My ways . . .

For as the heavens are higher than the earth,
So are My ways higher than your ways (Isaiah 55:8,9).

God's *timing* is not necessarily the same as ours. Even knowing that something is God's will does not mean it is His time. Joseph knew early in life that one day his brothers would bow down to him, and I'm sure he sometimes got impatient for that to come about. God had much work to do in Joseph's life and character, though, before he was ready for such an assignment. It took years of waiting before this dream was realized.

And David—he could have taken a shortcut to the throne by killing King Saul when he had the chance, but it wouldn't have been God's way. The Lord would not have been glorified in it. We must recognize that the *way* God accomplishes His will may not be the way we would do it. His method for accomplishing His will may take much longer than our method would. That principle was crucial to the process we went through in buying a house. We could have taken a shortcut and forced something to happen, but the end result would have been less than the best because it would not have been what God provided.

I like the way Jehoshaphat expressed this attitude of waiting in 2 Chronicles 20:12:

We are powerless before this great multitude who are coming against us; nor do we know what to do, but our eyes are on Thee.

He was facing the prospect of a war he couldn't win, and the only acceptable solution to him was for God to intervene. That is what waiting is all about. It is deciding, "I only want what God provides, no matter how long that takes."

After months of looking, Michele and I finally said, "Lord, we aren't going to buy a house until we are sure You are the One putting it together." After that we stopped looking and fretting, and just started waiting.

After about four months, we began to see God work. A pastor friend called to let us know that a house near his had just come up for sale. It was in immaculate condition and appeared to be a good value. We were skeptical at first but my wife set up an appointment and looked at the house. As soon as she walked in the door, it felt like home to her. It was the perfect house for us, in a quiet, older neighborhood, with a large fenced-in yard and beautiful landscaping. There was a fireplace (a long-time item on my wife's wish list) and even a pool in the back yard. It was three miles from our church and convenient to town. The couple selling the house had remodeled everything before they moved, including a kitchen that made my wife drool. It was everything we wanted and much more, and it was $10,000 less than anything else we had looked at! To top it off, God even threw in the down payment in the form of a surprise gift from family members. God's will was definitely worth waiting for! As we look back at what we would have been willing to settle for compared to what God provided, we know that His way is better than ours.

The Danger Involved

As we begin to get a sense of what God's will is, we are in real danger of trying to accomplish His will through our own efforts. I really believe that was the case with the house we tried to build. In light of our experience, consider the irony of Psalm 127:1: "Unless the LORD builds the house, they labor in vain who build it." When we put forth our own efforts, we may be tempted to take a shortcut. That was what Satan tried to entrap Christ with in the wilderness. He offered Jesus all the kingdoms of the world if He would only fall down and worship him. The funny thing is, what Satan offered Christ was God's will. Christ was supposed to be King of all the earth. The key difference was that Satan tempted Christ to have the will of God in an easier way, without going to the cross.

Do you struggle with such temptations? In your present situation do you desire to take shortcuts? Perhaps you sense marriage is in your future, but because of loneliness or longing you are trying to find a mate on your timetable instead of letting God provide one on His. Or maybe you are miserable in your present job and you realize it is not God's long-term calling for you. Are you waiting for the job God provides, or are you looking for the quickest exit from an undesirable situation?

The biggest threat to waiting is reflected in our unwillingness and in our lack of trust. If I really believe God's will is best, I should be willing to wait for it. If I don't, the problem is deeper. It may be rooted in a wrong view of God. Remember, His will is always "good, and acceptable, and perfect."

❑❑❑

Applying the Principle
Biblical waiting is not a passive response to decision making — it is faith in action. It is active trust in God and what He is able to provide. Ask yourself the following questions as you apply this principle of waiting:

1. Is there any evidence that God wants me to wait on Him before resolving this decision?

What is it?

2. Is there any lack of willingness on my part to wait on God?

How would I identify it?

3. What can I do while I wait?

14

Signpost #12

The FORK IN THE ROAD *Sign:*
The Sound Mind Principle

❑❑❑❑❑

S am nervously broke the lead of his pencil as he
scratched meaninglessly at the project he was working on. He'd been at it for hours but couldn't focus
on what needed to be done. His mind kept leaping back to
the decision looming ahead. The job offer seemed too good
to be true: a $10,000 raise, his own secretary, a company
car, and a job he could really sink his teeth into. At first
he'd thought of it as a blessing from God, but now he
wasn't so sure.

The new job would mean moving his wife and children halfway across the state, leaving their friends and family, and their church. It would uproot the kids from school, and Steve had just made the varsity football team. And it would mean switching to a rival company. How could he tell his boss that? Fred had been more than a boss to Sam, more like the father he never had. Fred had hired Sam straight out of college and had shown him the ropes. When Sam went through a rough period just before becoming a Christian, when his drinking got out of hand, Fred had been more understanding than most bosses would have been, even keeping him on salary while he went through treatment. *How do you balance loyalty with opportunity?* Sam questioned silently.

His neighbor had advised him to take the job. "No one stays with the same company as long as you have anymore," the neighbor had explained. "You have to think about what is best for yourself and your family."

"But is the financial aspect the only way to measure that?" Sam mused.

A few years ago Sam might have jumped at the opportunity. However, when he became a Christian, many things in his life changed—including his values and his dreams. He still enjoyed his work as much as ever, but now he realized that wasn't the only thing in his life with meaning. His family had become a priority, and he really got a lot out of his involvement at church. It had come to mean so much more than just biding time in the pew counting the seconds till he could hit the couch at kickoff. Now, he actually looked forward to the sermons; he even took notes, and he really liked helping out with the youth on Wednesday nights. Taking this new job would affect so much more than where he clocked in and who he answered to. Beads of perspiration speckled his brow as he entreated, "What should I do, Lord?"

A few days later as we met over breakfast, Sam related his situation to me. "Eddie, how can I know what God wants me to do?" he asked in candor.

FORK IN THE ROAD

The last signpost we will look at on our way to finding God's will is the FORK IN THE ROAD sign. Life hands all of us various opportunities from time to time, and we find ourselves at a crossroad where a decision must be made. These decisions aren't always easy, though, because they have far-reaching effects. One of my favorite poems is the classic by the American poet Robert Frost, "The Road not Taken." He uses the story of a man encountering a fork on the path he is traveling as an allegory of life. The concluding stanza relates,

> I took the one less traveled by,
> and that has made all the difference.

Do you find yourself at "Two roads diverging in a wood"? This is where Sam found himself, and it was his first significant opportunity as a young Christian to discern God's will.

The Sound Mind Principle

Sam edged forward in his seat with marked enthusiasm as I began relating to him the "Sound Mind Principle" of Scripture.

In 1 Timothy 1:7 we read, "For God has not given us a spirit of timidity, but of power and love and discipline." The word for discipline also could be translated as "sound judgment." In other words, God gave us a mind that works. If we are walking with Him, we don't disengage our brain — we use it. The key is *if* we are walking with Him. In 1 Corinthians 2:14-16 the apostle Paul explains it this way:

> A natural man does not accept the things of the Spirit of God; for they are foolishness to him, and he cannot understand them, because they are spiritually appraised. But he who is spiritual appraises all things, yet he himself is appraised by no man. For who has known the mind of the Lord, that we should instruct Him? But we have the mind of Christ.

"We have the mind of Christ" is an interesting statement, but what does it mean?

To begin with, who is the "we" spoken of here who have "the mind of Christ"? As you look back through the verse you see that the obvious answer is "he who is spiritual." In this significant passage Paul identifies the difference between true spirituality and what was being practiced at Corinth. The "he who is spiritual" is contrasted in the verses that follow to "babes in Christ" and "fleshly minded believers." These truths reveal that the more we mature in Christ the more we will experience "sanctified reasoning" — or reasoning energized by the Spirit of God, who indwells and directs us. The wisdom of God that I have access to through the Spirit gives me more than simply a light on logic; it shows me how to "abide in the vine" and use what God has provided through my relationship with Him.

The Place of the Mind in Following God

In our pursuit of God's promptings, it is important that we recognize errors awaiting us at each of the two extremes. One error we can make is to lean too heavily on human reason so that any sense of following God is lost.

The other error is to be so focused on looking for some dramatic revelation from God that we discount the wisdom of our Spirit-filled mind. We find the truth between those extremes. It is found in using the mind God gave us, while looking to Him for leading. As a child matures, he depends less on his parents' directives and leans more on their teachings. In the same way, a Christian needs to grow in his ability to make biblical decisions consistent with what God has taught in His Word, and not depend on his interpretation of some dramatic sign.

Bill Bright, in "The Paul Brown Letter," gives a significant illustration of this balance between using our minds and looking for God's leading:

> It is true that God still reveals His will to some men and women in dramatic ways, but this should be considered the exception rather than the rule . . . Philip, the deacon, was holding a successful campaign in Samaria. The "Sound Mind Principle" would have directed him to continue his campaign. However, God overruled by a special revelation, and Philip was led by the Holy Spirit to preach Christ to the Ethiopian eunuch. According to tradition, God used the Ethiopian eunuch to communicate the message of our living Lord to his own country.

The point here is not that a Spirit-filled mind is inadequate, but that it is incomplete.

Sometimes even the best decision from the available information isn't enough because that information isn't enough. Philip could see only the immediate fruit of his ministry in Samaria, but God saw the long-term fruit from the witnessing opportunity with the Ethiopian.

As Sam struggled with his decision, I didn't tell him not to look for dramatic leadings of God, but I wanted to get him to look also at the objective facts of his decision. With a Spirit-filled mind, we can trust our reasoning to "appraise" the situation as 1 Corinthians 2:15 puts it. But how do we do that?

To appraise the situation accurately, we need to apply the signposts we have already talked about, such as counsel, stewardship, providential circumstances, and so on. This signpost is different in that it synthesizes each of these objective leadings into a coherent, systematic form. That is why this signpost appears last.

Putting the Pieces Together

Putting the pieces together in decision making involves several important steps. We must take the time to *identify* our options. We must *qualify* our options by identifying the pros and cons of each. Then we must try to *quantify* our evaluation. This is done by attaching a numeric value, a priority or level of importance if you will, to our pros and cons. Finally we must *justify* our results, reconciling the accounts of each to determine if there is a strong leader. Let's look at how this works out.

Sam and I started through this process in his decision. We walked through it step by step, first identifying his options. As we started writing, Sam identified two options: (1) Stay where he was; and (2) accept the other job offer. This may sound fine, but remember our early look at the binary trap.

"One of the things to realize, Sam," I related, "is that God may have allowed this situation for reasons we don't yet see."

Sometimes it takes a decision like this to move us out of neutral. Sometimes God uses a situation to get our attention and then leads us in a different direction altogether.

Without the job offer, Sam probably would not have taken the time to evaluate his career.

"I would encourage you to include at least one other column for God to fill in if He chooses," I suggested.

When he had done this, I had him write a simplified statement clarifying each option.

Next we qualified his options. We wrote out the pros and cons of each option as completely as possible. This is not an evaluation, just a thorough, objective consideration of each option. And it may require drawing on outside resources, such as the counsel of others. It took several days for Sam to complete his list. He spent hours talking it over with his wife, and he even involved the kids in making the lists. He also met with his pastor and his Sunday school teacher. He finally produced a list he was satisfied with.

Next, we had to quantify his list, giving each pro and each con a number value from 1 to 5. For example, time with his family was valued at 5, being quite important. This was a pro on his present job, but a potential con on the other offer. Salary was valued at 3, not unimportant, but not all-important either. There are no standard numerical values — it depends on how important something is to the individual. Salary might be more important to others.

This was a laborious process, but very worthwhile. Sam said, "It made me take the time to think about my values and to take a long look at all sides of the decision."

Our last step was to justify his columns. We added them up and subtracted the numerical value of the cons from the pros for each option. This process translates subjective values into measurable criteria. As a result, Sam was able to see more clearly how much he had in his present job. Maybe the other job offered a bigger paycheck, but that isn't the only yardstick of a career. "If all that mattered was money," Sam explained, "there wouldn't be much meaning in it."

Sam decided to stay where he was, but the process showed him why he was there, and in the end he experienced the confirming work of God's peace.

Potential Problems

Like each of the other signposts, this one is not without the potential for mistakes. One of the ways we can be misled is by having too much of a calculator mentality. The benefit of the process is not in adding and subtracting but in thoroughly thinking through the pros and cons. We may conclude that a certain course is right even if it didn't win mathematically. Remember, our focus should not be on the numbers but on what God is saying.

The other potential danger with this signpost occurs when we aren't operating with a Spirit-filled mind. In 1 Corinthians 3, Paul indicates that the fleshly minded believer operates in the same dimension as an unbeliever. If there is unconfessed sin in my life and I am not filled with the Holy Spirit, I cannot use the sound mind principle, for I will be "leaning on my own understanding." I do not have the "mind of Christ" unless I am in the spiritual state of "he who is spiritual."

If you are uncertain about where you stand, invite God to bring to mind any unresolved areas of sin. Confess them to Him and repent of them, and then reaffirm your yieldedness to His reign in your life. That is the key to operating in "sanctified reasoning."

◻◻◻

Applying the Principles

This last signpost affords you the opportunity to wrap up your decision-making process. I hope that by now you have thoroughly defined your options. Take time to review these steps to the sound mind principle, and then work them out on the charts provided.

Step 1: Identify

Identify your options. Clarify as well as you can exactly what your options are. Avoid the "Binary Trap" — don't limit yourself to any either-or decisions. Make room for God to reveal something different. When you have done this, write a simplified option statement for each option in the spaces provided at the top of the chart.

Step 2: Qualify

List the pros and cons of each option. Don't worry yet about evaluating. Just write them down. Include also the counsel of others in these lists.

Step 3: Quantify

Assess the value of each of the pros according to their importance to you and to the decision. Use the numbers 1 to 5, 5 being the most important, and write that number in the value column. Quantify the value of each of the cons in the same way.

Step 4: Justify

Now total your columns and subtract the cons from the pros for each option. This doesn't mean you'll always be led to choose the winner, but the process will help you consider all your choices more thoroughly.

Pro-Con Sheet

OPTION #1 –

OPTION #2 –

OPTION #3 –

OPTION #1			
PROS	VALUE	CONS	VALUE
TOTAL		TOTAL	

OPTION #2			
PROS	VALUE	CONS	VALUE
TOTAL		TOTAL	

OPTION #3			
PROS	VALUE	CONS	VALUE
TOTAL		TOTAL	

15

God's Will and Your Life Mate

□□□□□

S ome who purchase this book will do so because they are trying to determine God's will concerning engagement and marriage. Perhaps you find yourself in these shoes. If you do, let me share with you some principles that are particularly relevant to the life-mate decision. You will be encouraged to know that for most of us, marriage will be God's will. But the other side of the coin is that singleness is God's will for all of us! Now, for most of us that singleness will not last a lifetime, but it is essential that we realize that singleness is not waiting for the will of God—rather, it is part of it.

Not Finding but Becoming

I think one of the biggest mistakes a Christian can make is to put all the emphasis on "finding 'the' one." You see, since singleness is, at least for a time, God's will for us, then He can and does use it for our good. I do not believe we will find "the one" until we become who God wants us to be. This means learning lessons from single-ness. When we *become* the right mate, then we are free to *find* the right mate.

What is the primary lesson of singleness? Is it self-control? Is it personal maturity? Is it patience? If your singleness is as mine was, you may see that the primary lesson is, you don't like being single.

But there is a far more important lesson that many people miss. In fact, I believe missing this is at the root of many problems that can arise after marriage. In 1 Corin-thians 7, the apostle Paul talks much about marriage and singleness, and in verse 35 he gives what I believe to be the primary purpose for our singleness: "to secure un-distracted devotion to the Lord." Before we can handle the responsibilities of married life, we must first learn what it means for Christ to be preeminent. Of course, we never stop learning that lesson, but if it is not made secure in our singleness, it will be much harder to come to that point when married.

Marriage is great, a tremendous blessing; it is a beautiful thing. I am so grateful for the godly wife I am blessed with and for the many ways God uses her in my life. But marriage isn't everything. It was never intended to be. Many couples are disillusioned because they enter matrimony with the expectation that their wife or husband is going to meet all their needs, and when it doesn't happen, they are disappointed. But God never intended our mate to be saddled with so great a responsibility. The only one capable of meeting all our needs is God. He can meet some of those needs through our mate if he chooses, but He is the one we must look to.

Let me illustrate what I mean. Take my desire for intimacy. If I expect my mate to meet that need and she doesn't, it will move me to sulk, or become angry, or demand more than she can deliver. If I look to God to meet that need through my mate and she doesn't meet it, that will move me to prayer, to self-examination, and to asking God what He wants me to see. He may be using that area to get my attention and to teach me something or to reveal a particular area of my life He wants to deal with.

You see, God must be at the core of our lives. Putting Him there is, I believe, the primary purpose for our singleness. It is an opportunity for undistracted devotion which then serves as the foundation for every other lesson we must learn — in singleness and in marriage, indeed in all of life. Once that undistracted devotion to the Lord is secured, then we are able to enter into marriage as we should. Our relationship with God gives us the ability to give what we should in a marriage relationship.

Making the Decision

As with any area of decision making, if I am not careful, I can err in one of two extremes: (1) by seeing the decision as solely mine and not seeking God's wisdom at all; or (2) by being so focused on finding "the one" God has selected that I don't take any responsibility for the decision myself. Again, the truth lies somewhere between the two extremes.

Is there only one person I can marry? I don't pretend to know the answer to that complex question. I do know, however, that God's Word limits who I can marry, and that He has unlimited wisdom for every decision I must make. Certainly, He is in the middle of so important a decision as this, and we must seek His will.

I believe that all the principles we discussed come into play in the choice of a life mate. Lordship must be settled. We must pray, search the Scriptures, obtain counsel and count the cost. This is a decision to take seriously. But we must realize that, especially in this arena, decision-making involves more than just gathering information or interpreting emotions. It also involves the will—I must make the choice to surrender my singleness and its freedoms, and to commit myself permanently to another person for her betterment and not simply mine.

If, after going through the process discussed in this book, you still have problems making the decision, let me share with you some helpful principles. They come from a seminar called "God's Will for Marriage," a special engaged couples part of the Family Life Conference, "A Weekend To Remember" sponsored by the Family Ministry. I strongly encourage all engaged couples and those contemplating marriage to attend one of these weekends. It will be an invaluable investment in your married life. My wife and I attended one about six months before we were married and were ministered to so much that we have gone back four times as a married couple. For information on the dates of conferences near you, write or call:

The Family Ministry
P.O. Box 23840
Little Rock, AR 72221-3840
Phone 501/223-8663

The following information on "getting off the fence" is from pages 57-59 of the Family Life Conference notebook and has been reprinted by permission.

Getting Off the Fence

Have you been "on the fence" for a period of time in making this decision? Have you been dating for forty years but just aren't quite sure if this is God's "one" for you? You may be lingering in your decision for one of several reasons:

(1) You may have a personal history of indecisiveness. Perhaps you grew up in a home where your decisions were always criticized by your parents and you have trouble trusting your decisions.

(2) Another reason might be that pain from past relationships or failed relationships around you causes you to fear making a commitment.

(3) A third reason for your indecisiveness could be that God is leading the two of you apart.

If you have been on the fence for too long, you each should get alone with God for forty-eight hours to help confirm His will. The following steps are suggested guidelines for this process:

STEP #1: Ask yourself if you are right with God. Confess your sins and humble yourself before Him. Relinquish all rights to your life to your heavenly Father.

STEP #2: List your fears.

STEP #3: Confess or acknowledge them to God.

STEP #4: Commit to God to accept or reject the other person as God's provision for your needs.

STEP #5: Write out that commitment to God.

STEP #6: Hold your decision privately for twenty-four hours allowing God to confirm it with His peace.

STEP #7: Tell one close friend. This allows him or her to confirm your decision and to hold you accountable.

STEP #8: Verbalize your decision to your potential mate.

After the decision has been made, it is important to protect yourself (and your potential mate) from backing down on your commitment. Once God has directed you, procrastination can lead you back to indecisiveness. So verbalize your commitment! If you decide it is not God's will for you to marry, it is essential that you make a clean break. The Family Life ministry strongly suggests that there be no communication between the two of you for six months. If it seems that God is leading the relationship back together, then wise counsel should be sought before re-establishing contact. Perhaps the close friend you confided in is a good person to start with.

And remember, God's will is ultimately known by faith.

Without faith it is impossible to please Him, for he who comes to God must believe that He is, and that He is the rewarder of those who seek Him (Hebrews 11:6).

Trust Him.

If you decide it is God's will for the two of you to marry, it is important to protect yourself from doubts. Bring doubts out into the open, discuss them, and deal with them as they arise. Become accountable to others for your decision. This will help. If either one of you is totally overwhelmed with doubts that he or she cannot control and the Lord does not remove them, the only option is to break the relationship. A broken relationship is better than a broken marriage.

16

God's Will and Career Choices

□□□□□

S ome who purchase this book will do so because they are trying to determine God's will concerning a career choice or change. Perhaps you find yourself in these shoes. If you do, let me share with you some principles that are particularly relevant to career decisions. You will be encouraged to know that God's Word has quite a bit to say about our vocations.

Contrary to what you may have been taught, work did not originate after the fall. Work was part of God's design from the beginning. Adam began his stay in Eden with a job description. He was assigned the managerial post of CEO of Creation. In Genesis 1:28 we read that he and Eve were responsible to "rule over . . . every living thing that moves on the earth." In chapter 2 we see this expanded. Verse 15 tells us that God "took man and put him in the garden to cultivate it and keep it." We also see Adam with the responsibility and authority to name all the animals God created. All of this is before sin ever became an issue. After the fall, sweat enters the picture — but work is not punishment. It is holy and meaningful.

In John 4:34 Jesus tells us, "My food is to do the will of Him who sent Me." I don't want to stretch this further than it goes, but think a moment about the purpose of food. Food sustains us and satisfies us. God put the flavor in food; man didn't. I think it is legitimate to say that God's plan for our lives will both sustain us and satisfy us.

Finding a Life Purpose

Maybe all you are trying to figure out right now is whether to say yes or no to a job opportunity. Or perhaps you are dissatisfied where you are and you want God to provide something else. Or you might be about to graduate from college and begin interviewing. Maybe you are in college, or headed that way, and are trying to settle on a major field of study. If you want long-term answers, it is important that you look beyond your immediate situation. In order to know what job to take or what field to major in, you need to have a defined sense of what career you are called to. And to have that sense, you need to go a little further and develop a life purpose. Unfortunately, many people I meet have no real sense of any life purpose. They see the only reason for having a job as being able to pay the bills. There will be little satisfaction if the only return you get from your career is money.

But how does one go about getting a sense of life purpose? First of all, the whole counsel of God's Word indicates that there is much more to life purpose than fulfillment of self. In the upper room, Jesus prayed, "I have glorified Thee on the earth, having accomplished the work which Thou hast given Me to do" (John 17:4). This statement reveals two important dimensions of life purpose. One overriding purpose for all believers is that God would be glorified in their lives. The Westminster Catechism expresses it this way: "The chief aim of man is to glorify God, and to enjoy Him forever." Glorifying God involves not just our work, but every dimension of our lives. Christ clarifies, however, that one of the ways we bring glory to God is by accomplishing the work He gives us to do individually. Our vocation is part of that.

Are You Called?

There is an erroneous idea floating around in Christendom that needs to be addressed. I meet many sincere believers who talk about "calling." They take that term from the references Paul and others make to being "called" to a certain ministry. The problem is, many people wrongly believe that if you aren't "called to the ministry," then God does not care what you do with your life.

Nothing could be further from the truth.

I believe you need just as much a calling from God to be a doctor/lawyer/Indian chief/butcher/baker/candlestick maker as you do to be a pastor or evangelist or missionary. Too many people use the lack of lightning from heaven or writing in the sky as an excuse to live as they want with no thought for what pleases God. Or they muddle along feeling insignificant because they aren't a part of God's elite. I believe God wants Christian doctors, Christian lawyers, Christian government officials, Christian businessmen and bosses just as much as He wants pastors and missionaries. Everything I read in Scripture prompts me to conclude that each believer is unique, precious and significant in the plan of God, not simply those in His direct employment. To suggest otherwise is contrary to Paul's teaching in 1 Corinthians 12 which shows us the necessity of every person's contribution.

Defining Our Diversity: Spiritual Gifts

Scripture is not silent about our diversity in the body of Christ. In fact, it shows quite clearly that diversity is God's design. Every believer is endowed with at least one dimension of spiritual giftedness, and I join many others in the belief that we hold several.

As we address the issue of life purpose, we must also address this issue of spiritual giftedness. Because all believers have at least one gift, and none of us possesses them all, spiritual giftedness helps us define what our life purpose is and what it is not. Personally, I have scratched administration off my list for life purpose. I learned early in life that I possessed little ability in this area.

But as one holding an "equipping" gift (teaching), I also knew that, whether as my vocation or avocation, I was destined for some form of church leadership.

Let me explain what I mean by "equipping" gifts. In Ephesians 4:11,12 we read:

And He gave some as apostles, and some as prophets, and some as evangelists, and some as pastors and teachers, *for the equipping of the saints* for the work of service (emphasis mine).

In this passage, Christ separates five areas of gift-edness and defines them as having been "given" to the church. The people in those areas of church leadership are put there to help prepare those in all other areas of giftedness for a useful place in God's plan. This helped point me in a focused direction of life purpose.

What is your area of giftedness? Knowing that will be a great help in finding where you fit. Although, from time to time, God may call you to make contributions outside your primary giftedness, your over-arching life purpose will lie in that direction, and there you will find fulfillment.

Conversely, if your vocation is not consistent with your giftedness, you will always have a nagging sense of frustration and incompleteness, no matter how much success you see.

Bringing It Into Focus

By now you may be asking, "So how do I bring my life purpose into focus?" First, you must realize that this is a time-intensive process. It will take decades to culminate. Although mine has much more focus now than when I graduated from college, I am still in the process of learning, still preparing, still growing. Fulfilling my purpose now is enlarging me for what awaits me. As I am faithful now, I lay a foundation to build on in the future. The key is not simply finding the right place, but becoming the right person. God's number one job with me is not changing my circumstances, but changing my character.

There are several keys to clarifying life purpose. First, we must bloom where we are planted. We must learn the lessons, accomplish the tasks and fulfill the responsibilities of the present before we are ready for the future. If you aren't careful, you may become so future-focused that you miss the purpose for the present in getting you there.

Second, life purpose is received, not achieved. God must open the doors for us. We must be faithful, but we are dependent on Him to provide the opportunities.

Third, life purpose is a process, not a point. The early steps I take in that direction will be pretty general. Later, those steps will become increasingly specific.

Bring on the Brass Tacks

Let's get specific and practical. How do you get from where you are to where we are talking about? First, *realize that your most significant contributions to life may be decades away.* Don't get in too big a hurry. As Miles Stanford put it in his book, *The Green Letters* (Zondervan, 1975), "When God wants to make a squash, He takes six months, when He wants to make an oak tree, He takes a hundred years."

Second, *don't bail out of where you are without a clear sense of where you are going.* Don't discard your education or present job just because things are tough. My advice is: Never simply leave something. Always be going *to* something. Don't leave your present job or place without a clear sense of God leading you to something else. If God wants you to leave, He is opening up something else for you. If you are the one wanting to leave, it may be simply because things are tough and your flesh doesn't like it. Don't make a rash, emotional decision to quit your job. Make sure that is what God is saying.

A third principle to keep things practical is this: *If you aren't satisfied, start praying and looking.* If we are walking with God, He can and does lead us through our desires. This principle doesn't contradict the previous one, but complements and balances it. There is nothing wrong with seeking God in our dissatisfaction — He may be using it to get our attention. But don't let that get you moving ahead of God. You must wait for His timing and His provision.

A fourth aspect of developing a life purpose is dialogue. *Talk long and hard* with your spouse and parents or pastor or boss *about what is important to you and how you are motivated.* God's calling is usually accompanied by a "want to" in us. We are motivated to do what we were designed for.

What Matters in Eternity

Finally, *hold your life purpose against the backdrop of eternity.* If your life purpose does not count in eternity, then it will be eternally insignificant. Regardless of how much money you make at what you do, if there is no eternal dimension, you are headed for a midlife crisis. At some point, your goals will be reached, but you will still be dissatisfied. The most frustrated person is not the one who fails to reach his goals, but the one who reaches them and then realizes they are the wrong ones. As one man put it, "I climbed the ladder of success only to discover it was leaning against the wrong wall."

How do we evaluate things eternally? Some would say if it doesn't have to do with God's Word or men's souls, it isn't eternal. But what in the Christian life doesn't have to do with those things? If I am serious about my relationship with God, His Word ought to be impacting my business practices. The Bible ought to affect how I relate with my coworkers, my boss, or my employees. God's Word working in my life ought to affect the quality of my job performance. Do I only witness door to door or do I also witness in the stands I take with clients, in the service I give customers, in the quality of the job I do?

For too long we have defined spirituality so narrowly that many see no spiritual significance in secular things. I am convinced that the line between secular and sacred is drawn not simply by what we do, but by how and why we do it. Conversely, the current epidemic of mediocrity is at least in part a result of defining that which is sacred in narrow, unbiblical terms. God can be glorified in the smallest task if it is done with His glory in view. Recently I picked up a book by Doug Sherman and William Hendricks entitled, *Your Work Matters to God* (Nav-Press). I was intrigued by its title because I don't think most Christians really believe what it says. It's true, though, our work really does matter to God, and we should involve Him in such decisions.

17

Conclusion

□□□□□

Recently I spent a weekend alone with my oldest boy Blake. We had many chances to talk without interruption, a rarity in a family of six. Over the course of those several days, I saw some real progress in what had been problem areas for him. I wasn't trying to make it a teaching time; I had no hidden agenda or ulterior motives. We just hung out together. We played some board games. We ate dinner at his favorite restaurant. We went to the mall together. We just had a lot of unhurried, unharried time. As I reflect back on that weekend, I realize how we both needed it. As a father, I had been doing a good job of communicating what I desired his behavior and priorities to be, but what made the difference for him was the relationship time. That gave him the "want to" to obey.

As I reflect on the will of God, I realize how essential it is that we don't simply focus on the rules of our faith, but that we work to develop our relationship with God. If that is healthy and in place, then finding God's will is not a separate pursuit but a natural dimension of what is already going on.

As we look back over the signposts, we need to note one point. The things we have talked about are not separate from our normal, daily walk with Christ; rather, they are the central aspects of it. Prayer, study of the Scriptures, the ministry of the Holy Spirit, the lordship of Jesus Christ, and our stewardship are all vital dimensions of our day-to-day walk with the Lord. When we have a need for wisdom in decisions, these aspects become focused in that direction — but only if they are already there. That's when finding God's will means less drama and less trauma.

The will of God is not a hidden mystery revealed to the super-spiritual or held only for a special event. It is an integral part of what it means to walk with Christ. As we have learned, though, finding the will of God is a process. Pursuing God's will is punctuated with points, but if we look at it only in isolated instances, we miss the big picture God wants us to see. It may be that the major decisions confronting us are there to underscore what isn't there in our relationship with God. As we wrap up our study of decision making and God's will, I'd like to isolate the key issues of walking in the will of God, not simply in finding it.

God Wants You to Know His Will

It is important to remember that God really wants us to know His will. Discerning His will is not a game of hide and seek. God never hides His will. Whether or not we are able to hear Him depends on how ready we are to listen. Consider this analogy. A father watching from the window sees his young toddler who has been playing in the yard and now heads for the street. He yells to the child to stop but the child doesn't hear. What will the father do? Will he resign himself to an attitude of, "Oh well, I told my will. It's up to the child to find it"? No way! The father will make sure he communicates his will in a way the child can hear and respond to, even if it means running outside and grabbing the child before he endangers himself. How much more will God, our heavenly Father, communicate His will to His children in a way they can understand?

Now, let's carry the analogy a step further. That same father will communicate his will a little differently to the older child or to the child who is hearing but not obeying. But the will is the same and the commitment to communicate it remains the same as well.

You Must Decide If You Want His Will

In order for us to hear what God is saying, we must be listening. We must decide we want His will, not our own. Until that issue is settled, we will make little progress in finding God's will.

Consider again the analogy of the parent-child relationship. The child who runs away from home and doesn't talk with his parents will not have access to their wisdom. So, too, if we are not in fellowship with God and walking with Him, to seek His will and wisdom in a decision puts the cart before the horse. We must first make sure our relationship with Him is right.

Of course, the analogy breaks down if you carry it too far. God our heavenly Father gives grace in ways no human parent ever could.

The Pivotal Issue of Jesus' Lordship

As I talk with people everywhere — in America, in Eastern Europe, in the Caribbean, wherever — I find that most Christians struggle with God's will at one basic point. More of a problem than our finding God's will is our settling that God's will is what we want. I have a will also. And when God's will and my will don't match, a decision must be made. I must answer the question: Who is Lord of this area of my life? It doesn't matter what I sing, what I profess, or what I believe intellectually. If I choose my will over God's, then in this area Christ is not Lord — self is. What I have seen as I counsel Christians everywhere is that choosing to do God's will trips people up far more frequently than an inability to find it, and that is where I struggle also. What about you?

God's Will and God's Nature

One thing that has helped me choose God's will when I don't understand it and it doesn't fit what I want is Romans 12:2. There we are told that turning from the world and cultivating a renewed mind via the Scriptures give me opportunities to "prove what the will of God is, that which is good, and acceptable, and perfect." As I look back over my Christian experience, I can honestly say I have never regretted doing the will of God. It has always been good in the end. I have, however, regretted doing the will of self. Every time I choose God's will, I prove to myself and to all who see that the will of God really is "good, and acceptable, and perfect." I have never seen it not be.

The will of God in any situation will always be just that: "good, and acceptable, and perfect." It always offers more than my will offers. It always fulfills me more than my will does. It will always, in the end, satisfy me in a way that my will never could. God's will is better for me than my own because of His very nature. He is good. If I struggle with the will of God, I am really struggling with the nature of God. It is no small wonder that the first appearance of sin in human history originated when Eve, through Satan's prompting, questioned the goodness of the will of God. Do I really believe that God is good? If He is, then so is His will. If I turn from God's will, I turn to a lie.

There is one incident in Peter's life that continually ministers to me. It was at a crossroad in the ministry of Christ. Many of those who had been following Christ had withdrawn from Him as His teaching and expectations became too demanding for them. Jesus leans over to the disciples and says, "You do not want to go away also, do you?"

Simon Peter pipes up and says, "Lord, to whom shall we go? You have the words of eternal life."

In essence Peter is saying, "Lord, if I turn from You, I am turning to a lie."

When I struggle with what I sense God is saying, I am reminded that He alone is truth. If I turn from Him, I turn to a lie.

What I have seen in my own heart is that once Christ's lordship of an area is settled, the will of God in this area is demystified. It isn't so difficult anymore. What I hope you discover as you deal with your own decisions is that God's will really is "good, and acceptable, and perfect." It is, but you will not discover that until you choose it. When you do choose the will of God, you will experience what you already know, the goodness of God and His will.

As you make those choices, others will be encouraged when they see the goodness of God's will manifested in your life, and unbelievers will see in you the attractiveness of Christianity.

My prayer for you is that you would know the joy of walking in the will of God, moment by moment! I hope this book proves helpful to you in that process.